Ted —

Stand by for an exciting ride — you can't make this stuff up!

Brian Orr

Love at First Flight

Adventures, Exploits, Risks, Sacrifices and Rewards

Captain W. Stewart (Bud) Orr USN (Ret.)
Fran E. Orr

ASTOR
+BLUE
EDITIONS

LOVE AT FIRST FLIGHT: ADVENTURES, EXPLOITS, RISKS,
SACRIFICES AND REWARDS
Astor + Blue Editions LLC

Copyright © 2012 Captain William Stewart (Bud) Orr and Fran E. Orr

All rights reserved. Except for brief passages quoted in newspapers, magazines, radio, television, websites, and blogs, no part of this book may be reproduced in any form or by any means, electronic or mechanical, including photocopying and recording, or by any information storage and retrieval system, without written permission from the Publisher.

Astor + Blue Editions, LLC
New York, NY 10003
www.astorandblue.com

All Photographs are the property of the Authors and are printed with permission by Astor + Blue Editions.

1. Memoir 2. Military families and their lives. 3. American Naval Pilot. 4. Personal relationships of American Naval Pilot. 5. Love Story despite the odds. 6. Heroism and Service. I. Title

ISBN: 978-1-938231-53-7 (hard cover)
ISBN: 978-1-938231-52-0 (epdf)
ISBN: 978-1-938231-51-3 (epub)

Book Design and Layout: Bookmasters

Table of Contents

Introduction vii
Chapter 1   Blind Date 1
Chapter 2   The Journey Begins 7
Chapter 3   Whiskey-Man 11
Chapter 4   Separating the Men from the Boys 17
Chapter 5   Red Light in the Cockpit 29
Chapter 6   Molten Metal 35
Chapter 7   Bad Boys in Hack 43
Chapter 8   Polar Opposites 51
Chapter 9   The Death Machine 57
Chapter 10   The Woman Worth Pursuing 69
Chapter 11   Gopher Holes—Not So Easy 75
Chapter 12   Jesse James 83
Chapter 13   A Rough Start 89
Chapter 14   Weird Harold 93
Chapter 15   Cross-Country Courtship 99
Chapter 16   Adjustments and Compromise 107
Chapter 17   One Night—Two Strikes 113
Chapter 18   Second Thoughts 123

Chapter 19	A Nuclear Carrier Wedding	129
Chapter 20	Night in the Box	137
Chapter 21	The Art of Partnership	145
Chapter 22	Tower Flower	151
Chapter 23	A Road Well Travelled	159
Chapter 24	A Cat and Trap	169
Chapter 25	Broken Habit Patterns	177
Chapter 26	Alpha Papa	183
Chapter 27	Another Notch in My Pistol	191
Chapter 28	Presidential Commission	199
Chapter 29	Final Flight	209
Epilogue	Charlie on Arrival	213
Glossary		215
Acknowledgments		219

Love at First Flight
*Adventures, Exploits, Risks,
Sacrifices and Rewards*

Introduction

Love at First Flight chronicles a generation of flying stories of one naval aviator and his wife. The story provides an intimate portrait of the magnificent fraternity of carrier pilots who wear the Navy Wings of Gold and offers insights into the women they marry. This band of brothers of the air is made especially unique by the awesome adventure of catapulting off of and landing aboard U.S. aircraft carriers.

Their women form indispensable friendships and support systems that provide encouragement when husbands are deployed. Aboard the aircraft carrier, aviators face challenges and the hardships of months aboard ship, separated from family and friends. They courageously risk their lives while representing our country in war or peace. During long separations families make the necessary sacrifices while giving steadfast support. Through it all emerges an unparalleled unity, honor and a sense of trust. Everyone has a job to do and most do it well.

In writing **Love at First Flight,** Fran and I have drawn on our personal relationships and experiences. The centerpiece of the narrative is the emerging love story told against a military background in which the love element is intertwined with my experience as a navy carrier pilot. The stories go beyond flying to the personalities and the families of those who fly. I am William Stewart Orr, known affectionately as Bud, and a navy carrier pilot. Senator John Warner of Virginia called Fran "the good navy wife" in an autographed picture.

The story unfolds with the roar of engines, the anticipation of flight, the catapult shot, the flight and then landing aboard the aircraft carrier which stimulated my senses and ignited my sexuality. My public persona was that life was to be lived fully. The world was my playground and "fight, fuck and go for your gun" fits most circumstances. Beneath the surface I was searching for that illusive something that would make me whole. My personal life had been tossed by the winds of fate, disrupted by divorce and separation from my young son. I was restless and discontented with myself and temporarily saved by my natural enthusiasm, passions and love of flying until fate intervened.

On a blind date I met Fran, *the woman worth pursuing,* a woman who seemed to be my polar opposite. We formed an unlikely union coming from opposing childhoods, yet the chemistry between us prevailed.

The stories carry historical significance and cross boundaries in time to provide a glimpse of the Vietnam War forward as the progeny of the World War II generation mature. Stand by for an exciting ride, a ride where you will go from zero to one hundred and fifty miles an hour in two and one-half seconds.

1

Blind Date

I WAS AWAKENED BY WARM, WET, sloppy kisses on my face. Sometimes I questioned why anyone would put up with such juicy kisses and bad breath. It must be love or I wouldn't tolerate them. I rolled over to avoid more expressions of affection and prayed to go back to sleep. It was useless to protest, as the Admiral of the Fleet—or Boo-Dog, my Old English Sheepdog—was awake and making demands for an early morning walk.

I was still hung over from another late night at the Lemoore Officer's Club and was in no mood to get out of bed so early. I remembered leaving the club where Rebecca, an occasional girlfriend, followed me into the parking lot and offered to drive me home. I vaguely recalled the short drive from the Naval Base to my apartment. However, I did recall Rebecca pouting when I asked her to drop me off in front of my apartment and purposely neglected to invite her inside. Rebecca was always ready for a good time and did not appreciate or understand why I said no to doing the horizontal cha-cha. I knew I had too much to drink and was in no mood for another meaningless tumble in the sheets, even with luscious Rebecca.

I had been restless and discontented since returning from a recent Western Pacific combat cruise and my wife, Diane, serving me with divorce papers. Thanks to Boo-Dog I was now fully awake and a morning run was much needed to clear my head from the constant reminder that I had messed up my marriage and was separated from my young son.

As Boo-Dog and I ran into the nearby park we were joined by Jim Maslowski. Jim and I were bachelors with similar gregarious personalities, good friends who also shared a passion for naval aviation.

Jim teased, "Cowboy, you look like you have been rode hard and put up wet, but you're just the person I wanted to see this morning. What are your plans for New Year's Eve?"

"No plans other than the Officer's Club. Will I be seeing you there?"

"Of course, I'll be there, but I need a small favor," Jim said. "I have a friend coming from the East coast for a visit. I was wondering if you would invite her out to celebrate New Year's Eve."

"Why can't you take her?"

"I think I have met the woman I want to marry. My girlfriend Billie Jean is special, and I don't want to screw up our relationship. I invited my friend Fran for a visit months before meeting Billie Jean. Billie Jean accepts my friendship with Fran but isn't happy about sharing New Year's Eve with another woman."

"Help me out here. Just what kind of friend is she?"

Jim attempted to explain. "Fran is a woman I knew a few years ago. She was strong and helped me get through a couple of really difficult times."

I said, "I recall a couple of sweet girls from college who helped me out." When we became involved the friendships ended, which was usually my fault. I'm attracted to many women but become easily bored, eager to move on to the next attractive female who caught my attention. "So okay, maybe I can help you out. But first, tell me what does she look like?"

Jim smiled. "This is the best part. Fran is not only stunning but independent as hell, and I know you like that in a woman. When we talked privately I always seemed to share personal thoughts with her I had never shared with anyone else. She went through some tough times but is resilient and seemed to never allow small setbacks to bring her down. She also has a partnership in a successful business in Virginia Beach. Honest, she is sexy and beautiful inside and out."

"If she's so hot, why didn't you roll in on her?"

"I thought about it, but the chemistry between us wasn't there. I'm just thankful we stayed friends," Jim replied.

Jim was in my sister squadron during my first cruise to Vietnam. He had joined the Navy as an enlisted man and was selected to the Naval Aviation

Blind Date

Cadet Program. Vietnam ramped up in the mid-sixties, and the Navy realized it could not generate the required number of pilots if it stayed with the requirement that only college graduates would be allowed an Officer's Commission before going to flight school. Jim had not attended college when he was selected to this program. He completed flight training in eighteen months, upon which time he received an Officer's Commission and his Navy Wings of Gold.

Midway through Jim's third cruise he achieved his hundredth combat flight over North Vietnam and was considered *combat limited* and sent home. Later in his career Jim received both his undergraduate and master's degree, was selected as a Blue Angel pilot, commanded a fleet squadron, and deep draft ship. Next he commanded an aircraft carrier, and then he was selected for Admiral.

Because Jim was such a good friend, I agreed to take Fran out on New Year's Eve. I also knew the time might come when he would repay the favor. Even though I trusted my friend I decided I would check Fran out for myself. If Jim was pulling my leg I just wouldn't show up for the date. I smiled, pleased with my clever decision to keep my options open.

I asked Master Chief Jones from my squadron to go over to Jim's apartment with a red rose. I had placed a single red rosebud in a small crystal vase with a note saying, "I'm looking forward to our blind date. I'll be the one with the Seeing Eye dog." Master Chief Jones returned to the squadron hangar about an hour later and said, "Boss, show up. She is stunning. A no shit ten!"

"Oh dammit," I thought, "What do I do now?"

Being ever resourceful I called my dependable friend Rebecca to help me out and asked her to go shopping with me. I hoped to impress Fran by wearing something special to the Officer's Club. If the squadron wore Navy whites with medals, I was guaranteed to impress her. However, Navy whites were worn on formal military occasions and would be unacceptable for the 1975 New Year's Eve celebration at the Officer's Club.

I could tell Rebecca was still pouting but hopeful for another chance for a non-slumber activity by the way she rubbed up against me. Reluctantly she agreed to accompany me on my shopping trip. After purchasing a pale yellow polyester leisure suit with an orange and brown paisley shirt Rebecca thought looked perfect on me, she suggested we go back to her place for a little afternoon delight.

"Honey, what I need is a real nap if I'm going to be up for a big evening," I teased and gently kissed Rebecca, patted the buttocks of her snug-fitting jeans and made her promise to save me a dance. I truly hated disappointing female friends, and I could tell I had hurt Rebecca's feelings by turning playtime down. I was on the verge of changing my mind but knew I hadn't fully recovered from being overserved the night before and decided it would be best to conserve my strength and energy for the evening ahead.

I arrived on time to pick up my blind date just as Jim and Billie Jean were leaving for the Officer's Club. I told Billie Jean she looked beautiful, kissed her cheek and asked her to save a dance for me. Billie Jean was a sweet, petite blonde beauty with a striking figure that attracted admiring looks like a bear finding a pot of honey. She caused heads to turn whenever she walked by, including mine. I smiled and winked at her, happy for my friend Jim.

"Here I go," I thought to myself as I walked to the front door. Fran was elegant in a black designer silk pants outfit clinging in all the right places. Jim had told me she was thirty-four years old but looked much younger. She stepped forward and introduced herself. We felt the shock wave as hand touched hand. Without hesitation Fran said, "Hello Bud, I am Fran Adams. I am very pleased to meet you."

I smiled, optimistic about the evening and thought to myself, "I'm one lucky son of a bitch."

All of a sudden my good deed to Jim was fortuitous. In fact it seemed like genius. I felt my life was about to change in a very positive direction as I drove to the Officer's Club for the New Year's Eve celebration. Fran appeared relaxed and confident walking beside me. I had good reason to anticipate an exceptional evening ahead. When we arrived at the Club, Fran and I took the time to enjoy and admire the gaily decorated lobby. I gazed up at a large mistletoe ball hanging in the entrance to the dining room and considered leaning over and gently kissing her.

I quickly reconsidered when my ever-present Censor stepped in with advice: "Slow down, you don't want to appear too eager."

In the background the band was playing a country western song where a singer crooned *"somebody done somebody wrong."* Friends and squadron mates greeted one another, anticipating the fun of celebrating the evening festivities.

Blind Date

I was outgoing, gregarious and well known at the Officer's Club for partying hard and being a fun-loving man. My first passion was flying and second was talking about flying or telling a risqué joke while being surrounded by an engaging male or female audience.

I made a valiant attempt to keep Fran close by my side but found myself with hands in the air talking about a pilot in the Replacement Air Group who recently survived a challenging ejection from his aircraft. As a landing signal officer (LSO) I had witnessed more than my share of accidents and close calls from the LSO platform. I was often asked, and happy to share my observations and experiences.

Fran smiled serenely across the room at me. As we made eye contact she let me know she was fine, could take care of herself and was enjoying the evening with my friends. I was pleased by her independence and ease in social situations. However, her self-reliance also made me a little nervous. I had plans to take Fran to my apartment later in the evening, with every intention of getting her naked in my bed. Thankfully I had remembered to make my bed prior to picking her up for the evening. I also knew several of my squadron mates were just waiting for me to screw up so one of them could roll in on her. It had happened before, but no way was I letting that happen tonight.

Once Fran and I danced together I didn't leave her side. We moved in tandem as if we had danced together for years. I was bold, arrogant and feeling very potent as I drew her close to me. I brushed my lips along Fran's cheek and softly down her silky neck. The jolt went straight to my loins.

> *"Does she realize how she is affecting me and the way I am aroused by her smallest movement?" I asked my Censor, who refused to answer. I thought, "How do I describe the way she felt the first time we danced together, the first time I held her in my arms?"*

I held Fran close and became confident that what I hoped would come true before the evening ended as she began to gradually yield her body degree by slow degree to mine.

Would I remember the evening as a momentary flash of pleasure, or instead as a catapult shot off an aircraft carrier going from zero to one hundred and fifty miles an hour in less than three seconds?

My hand moved from her hips upward, hoping she would allow herself to drown in the sea of pleasure I was feeling. She pulled back to gaze into my eyes, seemed satisfied and moved once again into my arms.

"Whoa, what just happened? You are going way to fast," my Censor screamed. *"What do you think you are doing?"* I pleaded for my Censor to butt out, *"I need this moment, I need her."*

If Fran noticed or felt my inner turmoil she gave no indication that she did as she gazed tenderly into my eyes.

When the song ended we continued to move slowly together, feeling the sexual electricity that coerced through our bodies. I was eager to leave and celebrate the beginning of the New Year alone with my incredible blind date. "Fran, let's go back to my apartment and have our own celebration," I suggested.

Fran laughed, "I can see where this is headed and no way. I mean it, no way. That was not foreplay we had on the dance floor!"

I insisted, "Honest, it's not about sex. I just need someone to talk to who isn't involved with the Navy. I just want to relax and hold you in my arms."

Fortunately for me she was intrigued and appeared to have responded to my suggestion. "Bud, I do want to know you better. It is noisy here and that makes talking difficult. If I go with you I want you to understand I'm not sleeping with you!"

I was thrilled to leave early, optimistic I could deal with her comment about not sleeping with me until the time was right. At that moment I didn't have sleeping on my mind.

On the drive from the Officer's Club to my apartment I talked about my squadron, the VA-97 Warhawks. They had recently returned from a Western Pacific combat cruise culminating with the Saigon Evacuation aboard the aircraft carrier *USS Enterprise* in 1975. As I parked the new Corvette (borrowed from a good friend) in front of my apartment building I leaned over and savored the soft, sweet, sensation of our first kiss. I got out of the car and walked around and opened the door for her. Once inside my apartment I poured Fran a glass of chardonnay before opening a beer for myself. I had soft music playing in the background and deliberately left the lights low. So began my forever love affair with the lovely Fran, a woman so different from myself and all the other women I had known.

2
The Journey Begins

I HAD SEEN DESIRE IN BUD'S intense blue eyes as we entered his apartment. In fact, I felt he was holding himself back from taking me into his arms. I found his actions sweet and was sure he was taking it slow in order not to frighten me. We were both Jim's friend, so I was not concerned for my safety. I was enjoying being in California and looked forward to becoming better acquainted with my fascinating date. On the dance floor I had felt Bud's strength and also his desire as he held me securely in his arms.

For several moments I focused my thoughts on Bud as he handed me a glass of wine. He was charming, fun and I had seen how popular he was at the Officer's Club. I questioned my bold behavior and the answer I received was at odds with my beliefs. I was reserved and cautious in my perspective of the world and Bud exuded enthusiasm and a laissez-faire attitude.

I thought about my personal journey that had brought me to my blind date tonight. The turbulent experiences of childhood have shaped my life into the woman I am today. One of the most important self-help seminars I attended, and the most beneficial, was Dr. Ira Progoff's Intensive Journal Workshop. Dr. Progoff was a physiotherapist who studied in Switzerland with Dr. Carl G. Jung.

I looked into Bud's clear blue eyes to see if he was listening and said, "You are only Jung once." He laughed, as I continued my story. Dr. Progoff taught his students through writing journals how to recapture major periods of their past. By journaling students were able to bring present life situations into focus and discover answers to the type of questions I had just asked myself. The Intensive Journal Workshop was a way for me to realize my inner strengths, look at new possibilities and discover resources and talents within.

I took a weekend course at UCLA in Los Angeles that Dr. Progoff gave before he retired. One of the men in attendance approached me and asked, "What would a pretty lady from Sweet Briar College have to write about?" Sweet Briar College in Virginia is an exclusive, prestigious liberal arts college specializing in women's education and was where he guessed I attended.

I simply smiled, "We all have a story." Wouldn't he be surprised to hear my story! A story I would share with Bud as our relationship evolved to the next level. My childhood was one I avoided talking about whenever possible.

In one of my journal entries I wrote:

> My brother and I faced several years of farm labor, whippings, fear, poor health, and constant moving and family chaos. We were tools of our parents to aid them in their survival. My brother and I struggled to establish an identity, void of living in a household with a father and a mother who did not seem to care enough to accept the responsibility of being parents. We were neglected, abused and rejected, not because of our own doing, but because our parents were not capable of accepting the task of parenthood.
>
> Our mother would bring dishonor to her marriage by having two illegitimate daughters while our father served overseas during World War II. After my mother's disgrace she disappeared and later returned remarried. The survival of the family was entirely dependent upon seasonal farm work, so we moved frequently throughout the San Joaquin Valley of California.
>
> As a young girl growing up in the San Joaquin Valley with thousands of acres of rich, fertile farmland, I accepted harvesting the vegetation as part of the natural flow of life. My world was bordered on all sides by a government migrant labor camp. As a child my home was the grim world of the government camps which gave life to the starving migrants who fled the Oklahoma "dust bowl."

The Journey Begins

Life in Linnell Camp was a major improvement over what had been left behind in Oklahoma. Aunts and uncles received word of work and improved conditions in California and joined the family in camp whenever space became available. Camp was the extended family, offering encouragement, comfort and protection. Just as wagons in the Old West circled the campfire for unity and safety, the same center of gravity was to be found in our new dwelling at Linnell Camp. Children wandered freely on the unpaved streets safe from harm and were watched by extended family members.

The majority of houses in the migrant camp were made of rough wood siding with corrugated tin sheeting on rooftops. Most of the houses had dirt floors and no plumbing. If a family was lucky, their home would have wooden plank floors. It was a curious sight to see women sweeping dirt floors. One wondered why they bothered. A large shower house with open stalls was located in the center of camp and was used by all of the residents.

Thoughts of cotton fields, grape vineyards or berry vines are synonymous with awakening in the cold dark dawn to go to the fields that are now the recollections of a time gone by. The dirt, the smells of ripened fruits and sore strained muscles are the harsh memories of my childhood years. As a child you worked and worked hard, or you accepted punishment.

My family had an innate desire to work and be productive. Hard work was as natural as waking in the morning. The combination of the plight of the wandering Okies and their pioneer spirit became a fuse that ignited a vital force in my life. Families were forced ever westward as outsiders, working the crops, migrating from place to place looking for somewhere they could call home. They would struggle on by instinct, knowing somehow that they would survive. They were a society with little pride, but what little they had was strong.

As children our world was isolated so we had no way of knowing we had anything less than anyone else. As a child one learned not to complain and at the youngest age to appreciate the smallest reward. It was years before I realized we were poor. In fact, we were the lowest paid wage earners in America and our standard of living was below the poverty level. Years later the labor leader Caesar Chavez announced that housing in Linnell Camp was not fit for the Mexican migrant workers who came from Mexico. The Mexican migrant workers came to labor in the agricultural Mecca of the

Valley when crops were ready to be harvested. When my family moved from our tent campsite into Linnell Camp we were thankful to have been given the opportunity to work and improve our circumstances.

My vision of the world was that of a migrant laborer's child, and my daydreams brought me comfort and a desire to follow my dreams. Dreams that one day I would travel to Washington, DC and walk in the path of our forefathers. Images of what life might be swirled like leaves in the wind inside my head. Respect for the greatness and foresight of the founding fathers captured my imagination. I was Betsy Ross stitching the American flag. Pride surged through my body whenever I saw a red, white and blue flag flowing in the breeze.

My thoughts were private so I kept my dreams to myself. Privacy was difficult as parents and children slept together in tents or in the one-room housing. The strong odor of kerosene and wood burning in ovens was a common smell. The pervasive aromas were sour and rancid at times. Odors emanating throughout the camp and sounds of sexual mating were natural but never discussed.

Tonight I let my thoughts settle and waited for Bud to begin. Before beginning he said, "Maybe my story about what happened on a combat cruise during the Vietnam War will help you to know me a little better."

3
Whiskey-Man

I began, "On a clear, calm day in April the *USS Enterprise* cruised in the Tonkin Gulf. I was on the landing signal officer platform, located on the port stern of the aircraft carrier with my LSO buddies. We watched and graded each pilot's aircraft landing following a day combat mission in North Vietnam."

Fran interrupted, "I would think you would be happy to see a pilot land safely back aboard the carrier after risking his life and not need to give him a grade."

You're a sweetheart! I understand how you feel and we are happy to see every pilot land safely aboard. As a landing signal officer we grade their proficiency in order to identify where a pilot may need improvement. So even in combat every pilot landing aboard the aircraft carrier is graded, day or night.

My squadron was en route to the Tonkin Gulf for combat operations during the unpopular Vietnam War. I was attached to Attack Squadron VA-113 Stingers. The Stingers were part of Carrier Airwing Nine (CAG-9). The famous first nuclear aircraft carrier left Alameda, California, and was scheduled for a port visit into Sasebo, Japan, before proceeding into the Tonkin Gulf.

Our port visit was the first time Japan had allowed a nuclear powered aircraft carrier into the country. The Japanese people retained painful memories of the justified nuclear attack by the United States on millions of Hiroshima and Nagasaki civilians due to the inhuman brutality of the Japanese warriors in World War II. As part of diplomacy and healing, the country allowed a nuclear-powered aircraft carrier to visit their ports.

Upon entering port in Sasebo the *USS Enterprise* was met by demonstrators protesting in the streets. They carried burning torches and anti-American signs and slogans. I was accustomed to protestors in the states carrying anti-American signs. During college at the University of Oregon I enlisted in the Navy Reserves. I would sneak out the back of my fraternity house in my bell-bottom blues, get into my 1951 Hudson Hornet and drive to my reserve meetings in Eugene, Oregon, in order to avoid the protestors. The protestors overseas were much more intimidating.

During our liberty port visit the carrier task force, including two cruisers, was notified of the attack and subsequent capture of the *USS Pueblo* by the North Koreans. The entire task force was ordered to leave Sasebo and proceed under fast cruise to the North Korean coast in the cold Sea of Japan. The *USS Enterprise* was joined by the *USS Ranger* with the *USS Yorktown*, first to arrive on scene. I was twenty-five years old and would spend my birthday on January 20 flying over the frigid waters. I would celebrate with freezing cold, blowing sleet and snow in high, rough seas while landing aboard the carrier.

The mission of the aircraft carriers and the accompanying task force was to project a warning to North Korea by our physical presence. The United States was demanding the release of the *Pueblo* and its crew. As a show of force the airwing flew day and night operations with full cold weather gear. We wore *poopy suits* to reduce exposure, should we be forced to eject into the icy sea. Wearing the bulky cold weather gear would give me thirty minutes after ejecting from my aircraft to be rescued or I would die of hypothermia. Thirty minutes was just enough time for me to inflate a rubber raft, climb into it and say a prayer to be rescued quickly.

We hated wearing the cold weather suits and thought a straightjacket would be more comfortable. Around the neck, wrists and ankles were rubber sleeves that fit tightly and caused me to sweat profusely. The *poopy suits* were designed with a hose attached at the waist. The hose could be plugged into a receptacle which was built into ready room squadron chairs while waiting my turn to fly. To keep us cool inside our aircraft the same *poopy suit* hose could plug into the console inside the cockpit of our aircraft. Once a jet engine was started the aircraft's air conditioning would keep my body cool.

Getting into and out of the suit took time and effort and was one reason for the descriptive name. I thought, "If I have to take a piss, I'll never get out of this thing." I learned that the hard way. If you should have a bathroom emergency removing the suit in time would be impossible and your flight suit would hold the proof.

After the United States revealed the status of the spy ship, and the seizure and subsequent capture of the *Pueblo* crew, the United States continued to express outrage that anyone would have the audacity to attack an American ship, let alone capture the ship and crew.

Fran said, "The capture of the *Pueblo* was headline news. I was certain the Captain and his crew would be immediately rescued."

"I was too. However, within a month the *USS Enterprise* and the *USS Ranger* were ordered out of the area and cruised into the Philippines for a port visit. Although not stated, clearly the decision to leave the area was made in Washington, D.C., for the carrier task force not to retaliate with military force."

During our port visit in the Philippines the *Enterprise* took on additional supplies before we cruised into the Tonkin Gulf. Every port visit is eagerly welcomed and cause for celebration, particularly after leaving the frigid waters of the Sea of Japan for the warmth of the Philippines. We hit the liberty port, partied hard at Cubi Point Naval Air Station and in Olongapo City, knowing we were headed into combat.

My squadron left the Philippines flying brand new Douglas A-4F Skyhawks. During preparation for my Western Pacific cruise the Stingers had gone with Carrier Airwing Nine to the Naval Air Station in Fallon, Nevada. NAS Fallon was a sprawling base with restricted airspace and numerous bombing targets. Fallon is one of the westernmost cities in Nevada, on what is referred to as the *loneliest road in America*, the stretch of road on Route 50 through Nevada famed for its remoteness. It is an arid agricultural community with the principal crop being low-growing alfalfa, and it made for a superb environment for military training.

Fallon, Nevada, was where I first met Lieutenant Commander Pete (Whiskey-Man) Payne. Whiskey-Man was an F-4 Phantom pilot and also the Carrier Airwing Group landing signal officer, the prestigious CAG-LSO. As the CAG-LSO he had the opportunity to fly several different types of aircraft in the airwing in addition to the F-4 Phantom. Whiskey-Man enjoyed flying the new A-4F Skyhawk with my squadron. He was masculine perfection, a tall, thin, swarthy fighter pilot, with all the cocky attributes every pilot wanted to achieve, and they became him.

I was the squadron landing signal officer in training. Whiskey-Man spent a great deal of time during our relationship teaching me the art and skill of listening to the engines of an approaching aircraft as the pilot attempted to land on the aircraft carrier day and night. He taught me to look and listen for the slightest adjustment to nose attitude, especially in close to the aircraft carrier's ramp.

As Whiskey-Man mentored he instilled in each LSO how critical it was to project a calm voice, under extreme pressure, to convey confidence as they assessed the risk to a pilot who was very close to death while making a difficult carrier landing. Whiskey-Man was the best of his time. Later I would become one of the best LSOs in the fleet, due to the great training I received from my mentor, Whiskey-Man.

From the LSO platform I watched a flight of four Stinger Skyhawks enter the break traveling low, fast, and turned downwind. The Pratt and Whitney J-52 P-8 engine in the new Skyhawks was powerful. However, the A4-F smoked. A smoking aircraft was extremely dangerous anytime a pilot flew over North Vietnam. Gunners were tracking the aircraft (even at high altitude) because of the smoke stream coming out the tailpipe.

A smart aeronautical engineer invented a chemical to eliminate the dangerous smoke hazard coming out of the small jet. The chemical was installed in a canister located close to the engine of the Skyhawk. We would flip a switch inside the cockpit of the aircraft when flying over the beach in combat. The chemical in the canister was then sprayed into the burner cans of the jet engine. As the chemical burned it would combine with jet exhaust and make the smoky exhaust appear smokeless. A smokeless aircraft was safer to fly during combat operations.

The Navy Department rushed to eliminate the smoke which was putting us in harm's way without full knowledge of the chemical reaction that would occur. The chemical caused a coating to build up inside the turbine blades, leading to catastrophic failure of the engine.

Whiskey-Man

When Whiskey-Man passed the one-hundred-and-eighty-degree position abeam of the LSO platform he lowered his landing gear and flaps. He decelerated to landing speed as the A4-F Skyhawk approached the ninety-degree position from the ship. On the LSO platform all of us listened closely to the engine of Whiskey-Man's aircraft. All of a sudden the engine was silent. As quick as you could blink, the nose of the jet pitched down toward the sea, a sea that was only five hundred feet below. The aircraft was almost straight down when the ejection seat actuated and the canopy blew off. The rocket of the ejection seat flashed and Whiskey-Man hit the water still in his ejection seat and before the parachute had an opportunity to open. Even though the aircraft had the most advanced zero-zero ejection seats made (meaning you could eject at zero altitude and zero air speed) the nose down attitude and vertical descent put Whiskey-Man well out of the ejection envelope.

We all watched horrified, knowing Whiskey-Man would not escape after his ejection seat hit the water and the aircraft plunged into the sea. Whiskey-Man was the first of many deaths I witnessed firsthand in over twenty-seven years of catapulting off of and landing aboard aircraft carriers. But this tragedy was Whiskey-Man, my mentor, my idol. How could this be? I had watched the traumatic accident from a ringside seat on the LSO platform.

As I finished my story I saw that Fran had tears in her eyes. I said, "It was late at night before flight operations were completed. A few of us occasionally gathered in a squadron stateroom for drinks after flight operations ended. Drinking alcohol was strictly forbidden on all U.S. Navy ships. However, the leadership seemed to turn a blind eye to this source of relief, especially during the Vietnam era."

We assembled in Ernie Christenson's stateroom. Ernie was a full Lieutenant, on his second combat cruise, a Naval Academy graduate and the son of an Admiral. He was a handsome, seasoned combat veteran. Later in his Navy career Ernie became a famous Blue Angel pilot. A natural leader, he retired as an Admiral and remains a close personal friend. But that night he was really tough. I sipped straight bourbon and began to cry ever so quietly. Ernie noticed, and with several other pilots in his stateroom he reprimanded me for expressing emotion over the loss of Whiskey-Man.

"Bud, we all have to fly again tomorrow and possibly others will not land back aboard the carrier. We have neither time to wallow nor tolerance for tears," and ordered me to leave the room. I wondered if Ernie had been raised like some British boys, who, their private schools, were taught shedding a tear or two was shameful?

    I cried after the tragedy and in similar traumatic circumstances, and probably so did Ernie and the other pilots. If tears were shed, they were shed privately. The lesson I learned was I had no monopoly on grief. Losing a friend or colleague was like an amputation and I would learn how to live with the loss. We each grieve at our own pace and deal with loss in our individual ways. At least I considered this the unspoken code among fellow naval aviators in or out of combat. Whether a loss happened aboard the carrier or at home I came to grips with the pain and did not selfishly impose the emotional impact of my grief upon squadron mates. Coming to terms with the finality of death was a tough lesson to learn at any age, but at twenty-five I felt ill prepared. Years would pass before I allowed my tears to flow unashamed from my eyes.

4
Separating the Men from the Boys

I LISTENED WITH TEARS IN MY eyes as Bud finished the story about Whiskey-Man. He wiped my tears away and gently pulled me into his open arms. Bud held me close, lowered his head and kissed my uplifted face with the gentlest kiss. The kiss deepened as I responded. His hand slid slowly down my shoulder. Bud groaned, "God, you feel so wonderful in my arms."

I looked into his clear sapphire-blue eyes, and this time I became the comforter and wiped away the tears. The progression into the bedroom was sweet and simple as we reached out for each other. What followed was a natural flow of synergy which would later scare the hell out of both of us.

Bud took pride in being a considerate lover and several times I felt him hold back from the swift climb to fulfillment. The exquisite moment came, eyes met and on some deeper level the mating became holy. We were alone in the universe spinning toward a union that would touch the core of our being as we came together. Something special occurred inside two people who behaved in an unpredictable way. It could not be ignored.

I had flown to California for a carefree weekend and to visit an old friend. It was to be a weekend away from the responsibilities of motherhood and my demanding career. As a single parent I was protective of my daughters and wanted them to have advantages that I never had as a child. They attended Friends School, a Quaker school that exuded a relaxed atmosphere with a loving supportive environment. I volunteered at the school as often as possible. I taught a class of beginner needlework and handicrafts to the children who were interested. The Meeting House where I taught was warm and cozy to the children, especially when a fire was burning in the fireplace.

I had recently become a partner at The Cage, a designer ready-to-wear boutique in the Cavalier Hotel located on Atlantic and Pacific Avenue in Virginia Beach, Virginia. Between the girls and work I had little free time. My partner was single as were the other women who worked in the boutique. My life was almost totally female centered. We did have a regular male clientele who visited the boutique to purchase a gift for their wives or girlfriends.

Before leaving for California my friend Jim called to talk about his serious relationship with his girlfriend Billie Jean. He arranged for me to go on a blind date with one of his friends. He said, "I told Bud Orr a little about you and he was willing to take a chance on a blind date." After what had just happened between Bud and me perhaps I was the one who took the bigger chance. Our blind date had certainly progressed into something more, and if I wasn't careful my heart would be at risk.

Jim had cautioned before our date, "Bud can be a charming and sexy rascal. He is getting over his divorce and separation from his young son and will be looking for a good time. You be careful."

I rolled away from the warmth of Bud's arms needing time to process what I had done and what came next. I knew I should leave and return immediately to the safety of Jim's apartment. However, my body was not cooperating with my thoughts. It was responding in ways to let me know it was not ready for the night to end.

Bud looked at me, "Fran, I think you're amazing, not like any woman I have been with. I want more of your natural sensitivity. Stay with me awhile and let me get to know you more. I am always willing to tell another flying story but for now I want to know more about you."

"Jim probably told you that we have been friends for many years. He came to Virginia last year when he was flying with the Blue Angels flight demonstration team. He invited me to the air show and as I watched I found the show both exciting and terrifying. The Blue Angels fly their airplanes in such close formations that it looked as if each pilot was exactly where he needed to be in order for the team work as a unit." I had to laugh at myself, "Who do I think I am to tell you about flying when it is something you do all the time."

Bud turned and smiled, "Your eyes were sparkling as you talked about watching the air show and the Blue Angels flight demonstration."

"My eyes would probably sparkle if I started talking about going to New York on a buying trip for my boutique."

"Tell me what it's like. I love to watch your face and the way your eyes light up as you talk. Your face is so expressive. I'll say stop if I get bored."

"Okay, you asked for it!"

On the last buying trip with my partner, Deborah, the weather was dreadfully cold. We probably noticed it more because we were constantly inside a show room and then back out on the street to go to the next designer's show room. We always stayed at the Algonquin on 44th Street which is steps from Times Square, Broadway, the fashion district and fashionable 5th Avenue shopping. It is also located near Grand Central Station.

We were up early in the morning until late in the evening looking for new lines of clothing for our boutique. We often ate dinner in the cozy lobby dining area. The hotel is near the theatres, and by eating in the lobby we could enjoy watching interesting guests leaving and returning to the hotel.

Our accountant had recommended the amount of merchandise we should buy based on the square footage of the store. Deborah is the real genius of the business and more creative and adventuresome than I am. She is always studying, reading and searching for new, upcoming fashion trends, materials and colors for each of the different seasons. Although I am more cautious and conservative, I am happy to model anything she asks me to put on.

I have gained her respect and she always defers to me before placing an order and often asks, "Can you sell the garment you are modeling?" Sometimes she needs to explain the fashion statement being made and why it will be popular to a buyer.

Love at First Flight

The outfit I wore tonight is special. The designer, John Kloss, won a Cody Award for the design. The Cody Award promotes and celebrates American fashion and is given solely to designers based in America, unlike the Neiman Marcus Fashion Awards. It is one of the most prestigious awards in the field of fashion. This year we were invited backstage before the show. It was fabulous to watch practically nude models raise their arms for a garment to be dropped over their heads and down their ultra slim bodies before walking on stage.

Pausing, I said, "Bud, I had a wonderful time tonight, but think I should be leaving. What happened between us was wonderful and I was wrong when I told you earlier that I wasn't sleeping with you. Even though I broke my own rule, I have no regrets. Perhaps we should stop before feelings become involved as I am not into casual sex, and there are three thousand miles which will separate us in just a few days."

In an earnest and almost pleading voice Bud said, "Please stay awhile and let me tell you why I love flying and about my first day carrier landing in a fleet aircraft."

"Okay, I'll stay for one more story!"

During the summer of 1967 I was stationed at Naval Air Station Lemoore, California, in the rich agricultural San Joaquin Valley and flying with the VA-125 Rough Raiders. The Rough Raiders were the training squadron for the A4-C Skyhawk. I was part of the massive pipeline of Navy pilots being trained to fly in Vietnam. At the time there were three aircraft carriers on *Yankee Station* in the Gulf of Tonkin, flying strikes into North and South Vietnam. The pilots also flew into Laos and Cambodia when ordered. U.S. aircraft carriers were suffering a tremendous loss of aircraft. The primary loss was of the single-seat attack jet, the A4 Skyhawk. The Skyhawk was carrying the most exposure and losses because there were more of them than any other type aircraft in the war zone.

The *USS Oriskany*, *USS Ticonderoga*, *Bon Homme Richard* and *USS Hancock* were older, smaller aircraft carriers with three squadrons of A4 Skyhawks aboard each carrier. The three squadrons each had twelve aircraft flying strikes into Vietnam. Alpha strikes were flown with as many as twenty to thirty aircraft at a time. Pilots flew in formation into Hanoi or Haiphong, dropping our bombs in unison, while dodging surface-to-air missiles (SAMS) the size of telephone poles. When flying to the targets we also had to avoid large to small anti-aircraft fire all around us.

In a nine-month cruise one airwing lost almost all of their A4 Skyhawks, not only once but some numerically several times. This meant the airwing lost close to one hundred aircraft and many pilots. Some pilots were rescued, some captured or killed. Fran, I read that during the Vietnam War more than one hundred squadron commanders and executive officers were lost.

With such great losses, there was pressure on the VA-125 Rough Raider training command to crank pilots out faster. I would go into the operations office and look at the names grease penciled on a Plexiglas schedule board. I would see what stage I was in the qualification process and what squadron I was scheduled to be assigned. Whenever a pilot saw *must pump* by his name he knew he had been selected to qualify aboard the aircraft carrier day and night. This was the final phase of training before going into combat. The *must pump* pilot would be flown to the Philippines to join a deployed squadron flying combat operations. He would replace a pilot who had been killed, captured or was missing in action. I was on and off the *must pump* list several times and I didn't consider an early deployment in any way macho. Many classmates who had *must pumped* had already been shot down, killed or captured within weeks of arriving in theater.

In the end, I was relieved that I was not *must pumped* but assigned to the VA-113 Stingers, who were just returning from a Western Pacific combat cruise. The Stingers would have a six-month turnaround before returning to combat. It gave me the opportunity to become acquainted with my squadron mates, train with the airwing and also aboard the aircraft carrier *USS Enterprise* before sailing to the Western Pacific in January 1968 for combat operations.

After successfully completing two or more weeks of two to three flights per day and night, we were deemed field qualified. The next step was shipboard qualifications and day and night carrier qualifications. Landing aboard the aircraft carrier day and night is the final graduation of a naval aviator. *This was what separated men from boys, Navy from Air Force, and made you different from any other man or woman in the world.* Your life is forever changed as you are all alone in a single-seat jet, no one to help or talk to as you approach a bobbing target that literally appeared to be the size of a postage stamp and you are travelling at one hundred and thirty-five miles per hour both day and night!

I remembered an unusual evening when I was a freshman in Grants Pass High School and my father picked me up after basketball practice. My father worked long hours and was extremely reserved in words and actions. He lost his father at a young age and as a youngster experienced the Depression and World War II. I regretted my father never had time to attend any of my high school or college sporting events.

On the way home from practice, I said to my father, "I watched a movie in school about military pilots and I might want to become one."

My father quietly replied, "Well if you decide to be a military pilot, be a Navy pilot, they are the best in the world because they fly off and land aboard aircraft carriers." Done deal! I thought his recommendation was good and took his advice.

As we were ready for shipboard qualifications half of the class was sent to Alameda Naval Air Station in Northern California. NAS Alameda was then home port to several aircraft carriers. One of the carriers was the *USS Ranger* and my first fleet carrier aircraft landings were aboard the carrier in an A4-C Skyhawk.

The half of the class sent to Alameda were identified as *hot switch* pilots, meaning the pilots would walk aboard the aircraft carrier in port, get underway and wait for the *fly aboard* pilots to land aircraft aboard the aircraft carrier. The *fly aboard* pilots would get six day landings (traps) and then the aircraft were tied down on the flight deck with the jet engine running and refueled. After refueling the pilot unstrapped, exited the aircraft and as a walk aboard pilot I would take his place. I would strap in, be taxied up to the catapult and shot off for six day catapult shots and six traps.

The walk aboard pilots on the *USS Ranger* got underway and cruised off the coast of San Francisco and into the Pacific Ocean. The *Ranger* sat under a fog bank for six long days. Eventually the aircraft carrier cruised south, almost to Mexico before the weather cleared and there was a high enough ceiling to fly aircraft.

After seven days of rough seas and heavy fog I was invigorated to hear the sound of aircraft overhead. Next I heard the crash of wheels on the flight deck as the first Skyhawk came down at six hundred feet per minute at one hundred and thirty-five miles per hour to catch one of four arresting gear wires. Immediately, the aircraft taxied to the bow and was shot off again. The pilot would get six day traps, exit the aircraft and allow a *hot switch* pilot to taxi to the bow and get six day catapult shots and landings.

We were limited to ten traps per day, so each pilot would get six day and four night traps the first day, and four day and two night traps the next day for a total of ten day and six night landings or *traps*. Only then were we carrier qualified in the A4-C Skyhawk. For us this was our graduation, the last event in over two years of training. Our reward was a combat tour!

I suited up in full flight gear in the ready room and watched my classmates on the pilot landing aid television (PLAT). The PLAT recorded every take-off and landing, day and night, aboard the aircraft carrier. Butterflies were flying rampant in my stomach as I watched and waited for my turn. Finally my name was called, "Orr, report to flight deck control for *hot switch*."

Flight deck control is a small office looking out onto the flight deck and located at the base of the superstructure on the aircraft carrier. Inside flight deck control a busy team of aviation Bos'n mates kept track of all the movement of aircraft on the busy flight deck. The bos'n mates watched as aircraft landed and taxied around.

The flight deck on an aircraft carrier is very loud with jet engines turning, and aircraft landing and taking off at full power and being taxied around. Due to the continuous loud noise, verbal communication is impossible. Flight deck personnel in colored jerseys use hand signals to communicate in an amazing display of teamwork, to ensure that each and every flight evolution is a safe one. Everyone has to know their specific job and also the job of every other person on the flight deck in order to operate in silence in what is clearly one of the most dangerous, yet majestic environments in the world.

Hot switch pilots sit on a small bench in flight deck control awaiting their name to be called and an aircraft assigned to them. Only a few minutes passed when I heard, "Orr 302!" I jumped up and strode toward the huge heavy metal hatch that opened onto the flight deck. I lifted the steel latch which allowed it to open and pushed hard and BLAST. Immediately all of my senses were on alert.

Fran asked, "What caused the blast?"

I see you're listening. The blast was the heat of jet engines turning. The exhaust hit my face and was carried aft by the wind over the flight deck. Next came the smell of jet fuel, the loud scream of jet engines, the screech of an arresting gear wire being pulled out by an aircraft just landing.

Then I heard the full power turn up of a jet on the catapult and next the BOOM of the catapult hitting the water barrier at the end of its stroke, throwing a jet into the air. The jet accelerates from zero to one hundred and fifty miles an hour in two and one-half seconds.

I had reviewed the model of the flight deck in flight deck control several times, and knew exactly where my aircraft was parked on the elevator, tail over deck, between the island and catapult number one. I walked slowly toward my aircraft until I was standing below the portside nose of Raider 302.

I looked up at the pilot sitting inside the cockpit. His oxygen mask was dangling from his helmet as he smiled and gave me a thumbs-up. He had successfully gotten his six day catapult shots and landings. After refueling he would exit the aircraft with the engine running and go into the ready room and wait his turn to *hot switch* and get four night catapult shots and carrier landings. He double-checked the ejection seat to ensure it was safe before releasing the Koch fittings from his shoulders and lap. He stood up, turned around and backed out of the cockpit onto the tall ladder next to the fuselage and climbed down. The pilot put his head near the ear of my helmet and yelled over the scream of the jet engine, "It's a good jet. Have fun!"

We quickly shook hands and I climbed the ladder, checked the ejection seat again, and threw my leg over the side of the cockpit. It was like getting on a horse. I placed my hands on the canopy rails and lowered my body into the tiny cockpit. My legs slid forward, down the narrow tunnels to the rudder pedals on either side of the stick. The stick was formed to the shape of my right hand grip. There is a trim button and a red bomb button that allowed me to drop bombs. It had a trigger to fire the machine gun. The buttons and trigger were strategically placed on the stick to be readily accessible to pilots.

The plane captain knelt on the ladder and assisted me in snapping my torso harness to the four Koch fittings that attached me to the ejection seat. I reached up, put my hands on either side of the small canopy, lowered it down and locked it into place. Instantly all of the noise of the flight deck disappeared. I could feel the small Skyhawk being rocked by the other aircraft taxiing past me on the way to the catapult. It was like being in a cocoon. The Skyhawk cockpit was so narrow that even with my relatively lean body both shoulders almost touched the sides of the canopy rails.

I directed my attention outside the cockpit to the plane captain whose responsibility was to give hand signals to actuate the flight controls, flaps and trim in various directions. He replicated with hand signals to show me the control surfaces were moving in the correct direction. I continued to move the stick and rudder in response to his hand signals.

At the completion of the plane captain's checklist, I gazed at the young airman who stood below my cockpit. He looked to be around sixteen years old. He was as proud of his role in carrier aviation as any pilot. Steam from the catapult was blowing past him. His eyes peered through his goggles as he gave me a crisp salute. I returned his salute and immediately transferred my attention to the all-important yellow shirt who directed me up to the catapult.

Again, with the use of hand signals the yellow shirt indicated he was now in control of the movements of my aircraft. All of the signals below his waist were meant for the flight deck crew and above his waist were meant for me. He knelt down and slid his hands over one another, the signal for the blue shirts to break down the chains holding my aircraft to the flight deck. He then signaled for me to move forward by moving his hands in a slow chopping motion in front of his face. He simultaneously gave steering commands to the blue shirt guiding the aircraft to turn the nose wheel. I eased up on the power as the aircraft crept forward and then turned starboard toward the jet blast deflector to catapult number one.

Modern carriers have four catapults numbered from starboard to port, right to left. Catapults one and two are on the bow and catapults three and four are on the waist or angle deck. The jet blast deflectors (JBDs) are flush with the flight deck and the large steel plates are elevated by huge hydraulic actuators and stop at about a sixty-degree angle. When an aircraft on the catapult powers up, the blast from the aircraft's tailpipe impacts the JBD and deflects the heat upward. By deflecting the blast, flight deck personnel and aircraft behind the jet blast deflectors are protected from the hot and powerful force of a jet engine.

I was next in line and watched as the jet blast deflector was raised and the aircraft ahead of me launched. I could feel the BOOM of the large catapult piston below the flight deck as the piston slammed to a stop at the bow when the catapult reached the water break. Next, the JBD lowered ahead of me—I could see the catapult crew in green jerseys who managed the aircraft and catapult arresting gears. Intermittently they scurried about the deck as the steam released from the previous shot streamed from the catapult track. Steam blowing back toward my cockpit was an uncanny sight. A sight I would see one thousand and thirty-six times in the next twenty years of my life.

The yellow shirt directed me onto the catapult track. With slow deliberate movements, his hands in front of his face, he crossed his arms and clenched his fists, indicating he wanted me to stop my aircraft. I eased the brakes on. Behind me the green shirt in the catapult crew lifted the heavy metal bridal that was attached to two hooks, one on either side of the aft fuselage. The bridal was then hooked like a "V" into the waiting catapult.

When the catapult fired the Skyhawk would be thrown off the flight deck going from zero to one hundred and fifty miles an hour in approximately three seconds with ten to twelve transverse g's to the pilot. The bridal would drop off at the end of the stroke, and was kept on the flight deck by a retaining line. The line was quickly retrieved by the catapult crew to enable them to attach the bridal to the next aircraft taxing up to the catapult.

Day carrier qualifications are thought of and referred to as great sport! Now I was about to get my first catapult shot in a real fleet combat aircraft, the A4-C Skyhawk. Within the next few months the aircraft would be replaced by brand-new A4-F Skyhawks that I would find myself flying combat operations in Vietnam.

Now my aircraft was under the direction of a squadron troubleshooter in white jerseys. He directed me to lower my flaps, set the trim and exercise the flight controls. My anticipation grew as the catapult officer took control of my aircraft from the yellow shirt. He made a gesture below his waist similar to an umpire in a baseball game when a runner slides into home safe. The movement was a command for the catapult crew to take tension and lock the aircraft down to the triangle in the flight deck. The two hooks on the back of my aircraft and the hook forward of the catapult shuttle were attached to the large catapult piston below the flight deck. The catapult piston was waiting to be activated by a huge blast of steam that had been built up behind it and would launch the aircraft.

Separating the Men from the Boys

The jet squatted as the Skyhawk was pulled down into tension. The catapult officer looked directly at me and was holding his right hand high above his head. He moved his hand to and fro rapidly with two fingers pointed upward. This was my signal to advance the throttle to full power. The jet squatted even more as the Skyhawk accepted the power, trapped by the triangle that held the aircraft onto the flight deck.

I did a final check of my instruments with the engine at full power and saluted the catapult officer, the signal I was ready to be launched. He took one last look around to make sure the area ahead on the flight deck was clear. He dropped down on one knee, extended his arm and touched the deck. He raised his arm to a pointing forward motion. *Here we go!* My left hand was full forward on the throttle with my fingers wrapped around the catapult grip. My right hand was cradled lightly behind the stick.

Each type aircraft has its own anomaly as to how it takes a catapult shot—sort of like a woman. Some aircraft you fly hands on, some take a natural good shot with hands off. The A4-C Skyhawk wanted you to cradle your hand behind the stick. As the jet accelerated down the catapult track, the horizontal stabilizer got the wind over its airfoil and dug in, which caused the stick to come back into my open hand. When I reached the end of the stroke, I gently wrapped my fingers around the stick and held that position until the aircraft assumed a proper fly away attitude.

Then I got busy. I made a quick right clearing turn to get away from the waist catapults and raised the landing gear and flaps. I then eased the stick forward to accelerate two hundred feet off the water. I needed to make sure I didn't climb up to the altitude reserved for returning aircraft already in the break and about to land back aboard the aircraft carrier.

I made the call, "302 airborne." God what a rush! It doesn't get better than this!

5
Red Light in the Cockpit

IN THE MIDDLE OF THE NIGHT I awakened contented, amazed at how good I felt. It had been perfect to fall asleep with Fran in my arms. I enjoyed her explosive sweetness as we became lost in caress after caress. Everything was new and exciting. The story I had told her about day carrier qualifications had revealed my best reflected in her eyes. I wanted to share the exhilaration, terror and intensity of a night landing aboard the aircraft carrier, not only the first one, but every single night catapult launch and carrier landing! Now that the proverbial cork was out of the bottle, I looked forward to sharing more of myself with the woman lying beside me.

    I gently kissed Fran, who was deep asleep, until she began to awaken. As her beautiful sleepy green eyes slowly opened, she was unclear as to what had disturbed her sleep. Although I felt a little foolish for waking her I whispered, "I woke up with a beautiful woman lying beside me. You bring joy and laughter into my life and being with you is perfect on so many different levels. I want you to know me even better. Are you ready for another adventure?" Fran looked up with an alluring expression and moved her leg sensuously inside of mine. Her seductive body movements immediately distracted me. In order to put just a little distance between us I propped my head up on one hand and looked down at her saying, "I may be out of my mind to just want to talk right now but may I tell you about the exhilaration and intensity of a night carrier landing?" Fran looked up at me as if she understood my need to talk, and magically was alert and gave me her full attention.

What I didn't share with Bud was how unusual it was to spend the night with a man and how deeply I had been sleeping. At home I was a light sleeper, and when I awakened I would usually recall dreams. I was interested enough to take several courses at the Virginia Beach Association for Research and Enlightenment. Besides Dr. Progoff I had heard speakers and authors who offered various perspectives on dreams and visualization. I read several books on dream interpretations and had a journal to write down my dreams and thoughts.

My daughters were interested or at least curious enough to climb into bed with me on the weekends to share their dreams. Listening to them talk had become a unique way of bonding and gaining insights into their well-being.

I would think later about why I was sleeping so soundly with a man whom I really knew so little about. There would be time to analyze my dreams when I returned home. Bud wanted to talk and I was happy to listen and discover more about him. I sat up in bed with a couple of pillows propped behind my head and said, "I'm learning so much about you, not just your passion for flying and how vivid you make every story, but also the extraordinary skill and undaunted courage required of aviators. Now that I am awake, let's hear about the thrill of a night catapult shot off the aircraft carrier."

I gently kissed Fran and began to tell her about one of the most nerve-wracking times I experienced as a new pilot. I explained, "Landing aboard an aircraft carrier during the day time was only one phase of carrier qualifications. Far more challenging and dangerous was each and every night carrier landing. The process began very similar to the daytime *hot switch*. I was called up to flight deck control as a *hot switch* pilot. Just as in the daytime, I sat on a small bench in flight deck control with familiar activities happening on the flight deck. I listened for my name to be called and wondered what awaited me. All of the training and discipline I had gone through prepared me for the challenges and intensity of flight operations at night aboard the aircraft carrier."

The speaker system called out, "Orr 307." My heart skipped a beat as I cautiously stepped into the darkness of the flight deck. A warm breeze of steam rose from the catapult track. I could hear the now familiar scream of jet engines taking off and landing and also the eerie scene of yellow shirts directing aircraft about the flight deck with illuminated hand held wands.

I made my way to my *hot switch* aircraft, just as I had done in the daytime. *I realized this was a whole new game. This was the big boys club!* I was about to get into a small jet fighter at night, with no horizon, below a fog bank, and be shot off the catapult into total darkness, to be vectored around by radar into the landing pattern for my first night carrier landing. This would be my defining moment!

With adrenaline pumping throughout my body I experienced the same ritual of *hot seat* with the aircraft's previous pilot. After he exited the cockpit I climbed aboard, strapped in and checked the gauges in the Douglas A4-C Skyhawk. My aircraft appeared to be functioning well. Steam was blowing mysteriously near the small cockpit, which was being rocked to and fro by the blast of aircraft launches, recovery and taxiing aircraft. I sat mesmerized in a state of sheer terror and exhilaration.

The yellow shirt signaled below his waist with his lighted wands in a crossing motion for the blue shirts to break down the chains on the aircraft. After the chains were removed, the yellow shirt took control again. I looked out of the cockpit window at the yellow shirt giving directions with his lighted wands. He signaled for me to taxi my aircraft forward by moving his wands slowly open and closed in front of his face.

Then, with a graceful but forceful movement, the yellow shirt pointed his left wand down to the flight deck, an indication he wanted a hard right turn. I initiated the hard turn by gently applying the right brake. The aircraft moved forward on the flight deck toward the jet blast deflector behind catapult number one. The plane captain attached the nose tow bar to the aircraft's nose wheel as had been done in the daytime.

As I taxied the aircraft slowly forward, the jet blast deflectors were lowered after the launch of the aircraft ahead of me and a huge cloud of steam enveloped my aircraft as it was discharged from the just completed catapult shot. When the steam dissipated I could see the yellow shirt directing me onto the catapult track. I continued to move slowly forward until about mid catapult track, at which time the yellow shirt crossed his lighted wands indicating he wanted me to stop right now!

I immediately pressed the front of my steel-toe flight boots hard against the top of the rudder petals to activate the brakes. We wore steel-toe boots in the Skyhawk as a precautionary measure. I would slide my legs into tunnels and straddle the stick inside the cockpit. If I was ejected from the aircraft the steel toe of my boots would prevent my toes from being cut off should they impact the aircraft's instrument panel during the ejection.

I pushed hard again on the brakes of the Skyhawk. The rapid deceleration caused the long nose strut on the A4 to compress and the nose of the aircraft bowed toward the flight deck nearly a foot as the long strut of the nose wheel retracted. To my shock and horror, I had a red light in the cockpit which could only be bad news!"

"Were you scared?" Fran asked.

"Hell yes I was scared, but let me back up a minute! I was in a single-seat fighter, moments from my first night catapult shoot, feet from being launched off the catapult and my cockpit was literally filled with red. All I could see was RED." I instinctually keyed the radio button on the inside of the throttle quadrant and with a great amount of distress in my voice was able to squeak, "I've got a red light in the cockpit, and that's not right!"

The Air Boss in the tower, who controlled all flight operations on the flight deck, calmly spoke into his mike, "307 check your radar altimeter light."

Sure enough, when I looked down at the tiny radar altimeter light that illuminated the cockpit of the Skyhawk I saw the light was on. When the previous pilot had exited the aircraft he had set the preset attitude to activate. As I applied the brakes on the A4 the light was activated when the radar altimeter on the instrument panel recognized the flight deck. I was extremely embarrassed and momentarily felt like ejecting!

After the terrifying emotional episode over the red light, I had so much adrenaline pumping throughout my body that my first night catapult shot was sweet relief and without additional drama.

Instead of saluting the catapult officer to signal I was ready to launch as you do in the day time, I used my left hand to hold the throttle at full power, checked my instruments to make sure they were normal and with my little finger flicked the small switch outboard on the throttle to turn on the navigation lights. I watched the catapult officer make a final slow scan around the flight deck and aircraft as the steam majestically streamed about him. Then he dropped down on one knee and gracefully touched the deck with his yellow wand.

Now, the anticipated exhilaration! The aircraft squatted, and then accelerated from zero to one hundred and fifty miles per hour travelling less than two hundred feet in approximately three seconds. My head was pressed deep into the crease of the headrest of the ejection seat. When I reached the end of the stroke, just as in the daytime, the stick gently and automatically moved aft to find the palm of my right hand waiting for it. My fingers wrapped tightly around the stick and instead of looking forward out of the cockpit, which was total darkness, my eyes were fixated on two instruments. First, I focused on the attitude gyro indicator in the center of the instrument panel. Second, I looked just below the attitude gyro indicator to the right on the panel at my vertical speed indicator. At the end of the stroke the Skyhawk achieved the maximum g-load.

"What's a g-load, Bud?" Fran asked.

Just to be graphic, I threw myself on top of her body and lay there quietly. I said, "I'm one hundred and seventy pounds and you are experiencing my body weight at one gravitational force, or one g. Imagine it being nine times that force. Stop squirming or I won't be able to finish my story."

Often the g-load is so high that the blood in a pilot's eyes is pushed to the back of his retina, causing tunnel vision or sometimes a momentary blackout. A pilot recovers quickly from tunnel vision or momentary blackout because of being in peak physical condition. I would then immediately set the attitude of the aircraft on the gyro at three to four degrees above the horizon, scan to make sure my wings showed level and take a quick look at my vertical speed indicator to ascertain that I was in fact climbing away from the water, and then and only then reach down with my left hand and raise the landing gear and report on the radio, "307 airborne."

After I finished my story I told Fran I had been asked to give a brief aboard the aircraft carrier to visiting dignitaries who had brought along their teenage sons. At the end of my telling the group of visitors about the thrill, exhilaration and challenges of a night catapult shot, I happened to look over at the teenagers who had hung onto my every word. I smiled mischievously into the teenagers' eyes and said, "Some pilots think that every night catapult shot is equal to making love to a beautiful woman, and I'm not saying they're wrong!"

I was confused how one minute Bud would talk about the terror and the exhilaration of flying and the next minute relate it somehow to a woman's body. I had to ask, "Are you one of the pilots who think a night catapult shot is equal to making love to a beautiful woman?"

Bud looked at me with a puzzled expression on his face, "Do you take everything literally?"

"Not usually," I answered.

"Fran, there are moments with you that are better than my most exciting catapult shot and I can hardly wait to do it again. In some ways it is similar to what I feel when I strap into a jet. It is the unknown, the unpredictably, the risk that makes me anticipate an incredible ride."

I listened intently but also watched his body movements as he attempted to help me understand. At the time I thought being catapulted off of an aircraft carrier into the darkness was something I would never chose. It wasn't on my list of things to do in this lifetime and more accurately would be on my list of things to avoid. My list was more tangible, and I had already achieved many of them. Surprisingly, awaiting me in the future was exactly that, a catapult shot and carrier landing aboard the *USS Midway*.

6
Molten Metal

I WAS CAPTIVATED BY THE THRILL of Bud's catapult shot and the exhilaration of flying off the aircraft carrier at night. When he finished his story he edged closer to me, as though we had shared something intimate and exciting together. He moved forward, his lips relaxed, inviting, as he gently kissed me. As I leaned forward, I could not help but notice him looking down at the soft swell of my breasts. I responded to the sweet sensation and warmth of his hands touching me in a gentle embrace. "Was every kiss an act of love? Was love being born moment by moment?" I asked myself before becoming lost in his arms.

All of a sudden the excitement and thrill of his catapult shot was gone and replaced by the need and urgency to allow him to kiss me deeply, as my body yielded to his closeness. We blended together as one. Our joining was passionate, exhilarating as a catapult shot. Our natural response was a crescendo of caring and tenderness mixed with pulsating desire. The effect was as explosive.

I awakened before dawn and returned to my friend Jim's apartment. The flying stories and the man were exciting but I was exhausted from being up most of the night and left to get some rest.

The next morning I heard the telephone ring. Jim answered and immediately hung up the phone. It was Bud who called again and said, "Don't hang up. Wake Billie Jean and Fran and let's take a drive over to the coast. I'll see you in thirty minutes," and hung up before Jim could respond.

Thirty minutes later Bud drove up in the borrowed, shiny Corvette with the V-8 engine rumbling like the growl of a wild beast. I was pleased to see him and stood in the doorway, smiling affectionately. I was delighted he wanted to see me again. He sat inside the sports car, intimidating in his snug, faded jeans, white tee shirt and black leather jacket. His eyes were covered with dark aviator glasses. Even with his sunglasses, I remembered the clear sapphire blue color of his eyes, as clear as a spring lake, and a mouth that was quick to turn into a smile, a smile which continued to suggest there was no one he would rather be with than me.

"Let's go for a drive to the coast. I need to slow down and relax. I promise you a nice easy ride," Bud's voice was deliciously suggestive. I knew I was doomed as he continued to smile his reassurance that keeping me safe was of primary importance. He opened the door and told me to slide my gorgeous legs into the bucket seat and buckle up.

Jim and Billie Jean had other plans for the day and waved good-bye as the Corvette roared to life and carried Bud and me into the Coalinga Hills and over to the Pacific coast. It was a cool clear morning, warm for that time of year in the Valley. Bud cruised carefully through the foothills with me sitting by his side relaxed and happy. The drive was enjoyable, with the terrain a mixture of field crops that do not require large amounts of water. Numerous oil wells dotted the countryside where oil had been pumped for more than a hundred years. The area was also located near an active portion of the San Andreas Fault, where small earthquakes occurred with some frequency.

As we drove, Bud said, "I was surprised to awaken this morning and discover I had slept soundly for the first time in weeks. I rolled over to let you know I think you are good for me only to discover you were gone. The thought of spending the day without you was not an option."

On the way to Pismo Beach we passed through San Luis Obispo on the central coast, one of California's oldest communities. National Geographic referred to San Luis Obispo as *The Happiest City in America*. With an overall relaxing environment it is easy to get to and hard to leave. San Luis Obispo is on US Route 101 and California State Highway 1 and is a popular tourist stop because of the cool Mediterranean climate. Eighty-degree temperatures during the winter months were not uncommon. We drove past the famous Madonna Inn where each room had a different and unusual theme. It was a favorite spot for newlyweds and guests. Bud shared with me that he had spent a weekend at the Inn after being transferred to the naval air station in Lemoore. He asked, "Guess what theme the room I stayed in had?"

"My guess would be some macho type caveman room." He laughed, taken aback that I had guessed correctly.

We arrived in Pismo Beach and stopped to have lunch at the charming Sea Cliff Restaurant. We sat at an outside table watching waves crash over the sandy shoreline. Pismo Beach was picturesque and beautiful, overlooking some of the world's most pristine beaches, drenched in sunshine nearly year round.

Bud had promised to tell me a flying story after finishing our lunch. We wandered down to the beach and found a quiet spot where we would be comfortable while he told me about another adventure.

I was aboard the Interim Sea Control Ship, *USS Guam*, about one hundred miles off the South Carolina coast on a warm balmy summer night. Occasional lightening was visual in the distance. I was flying a British AV-8A Harrier, powered by a Rolls-Royce Pegasus engine as part of the first Marine Harrier squadron, VMA-513 Flying Nightmares. The AV-8A was basically an experimental aircraft, delivered directly from England. It was a unique aircraft which could lift off vertically, unlike conventional jets. The aircraft had poor instrumentation for night and inclement weather flight, similar to the weather I could see in the distance. The AV-8A didn't have a radar altimeter and had a simple push-to-cage gyro.

Fran stopped me and asked, "Is it important that I understand what a push-to-cage gyro does?"

"It would be helpful. It is simply a gyroscope, a wheel or disk mounted to spin about an axis that is free to turn in various directions. The gyro in the Harrier was primitive but was helpful at night to locate the horizon. However, it is more important to know that in flight the Harrier was aerodynamically negatively unstable in certain regimes due to its design. The AV-8A had a proclivity to fly upside down and backwards whenever it became negatively unstable."

I was flying at twelve hundred feet above the water, below a low cloud deck, with no radar altimeter. When I was ten miles from the *USS Guam,* I selected the nozzles on the Harrier to sixty degrees, to allow a semi-jet borne flight at one hundred and fifty knots or one hundred and seventy four miles per hour. The *USS Guam* was a converted landing platform helicopter carrier (LPH-9) and was used by the Marines to validate short take-off and vertical landing flight operations from the flight deck of a small carrier. The nautical term used for short take-off and vertical landings by the AV-8A Harrier is STOVL.

The landing evolution for the Harrier was designed to fly at twelve hundred feet, at one hundred and fifty knots. The AV-8A was semi-jet borne with the nozzles at sixty degrees down when I arrived at a point three miles behind the *Guam*. Next, I descended to six hundred feet on instruments with no radar altimeter until the aircraft was one mile from the ship. At one mile, I intercepted a three-degree glide path, lowered the nozzles to ninety degrees and began decelerating the aircraft.

Keep in mind, the ninety- to thirty-knot range was always treacherous! I mentioned previously that when a Harrier entered the negative stability range the aircraft had a proclivity to fly upside down and backwards. Now, add nighttime into the equation, over the water, no horizon, and a small ship to land aboard.

Easing gently back on the stick reduced airspeed naturally as the aircraft slowed. With less air flow over the wing the Harrier started depleting wing-lift. Wing-lift must inevitably be replaced with jet-borne lift provided by thrust from the four power poles of jet thrust blowing straight down out of the Pegasus engine. Another key element to the evolution was the ninety-knot or one hundred and five miles per hour airspeed queue. This could only be noted by scanning the airspeed indicator as the Harrier dropped through ninety knots. Dropping below the ninety-knot range was important because below ninety knots there was a rapid depletion of wing-lift, called *wing-wash*.

Wing-wash meant the Harrier was very quickly depleting wing-lift as the aircraft slowed below that airspeed. To compensate for the depleting wing-lift at the ninety-knot queue, I was trained to add a handful of power. Adding power would spool up the twenty thousand pounds of thrust Rolls-Royce Pegasus engine to about ninety-two percent power. The vertical lift from the nozzle power poles pointing straight down replaced the wing-lift lost by the deceleration and subsequent *wing-wash*.

Well, not so fast there, *Squid*. The Marines had chosen *Squid* as my call sign during the beginning of my exchange tour for obvious reasons. I was totally engaged with the aircraft, tossing around in the bumpy, lightening shrouded, warm summer air. The nose of the aircraft was bouncing up and down, left and right, now dangerously so. If the nose of the Harrier got too far out of the relative wind, the AV-8A would quickly flip upside down and crash.

I was totally distracted by the extremely high cockpit workload caused by jostling around in the sky. I missed the queue as the aircraft quickly decelerated through ninety knots. The Harrier literally floated up to a point one-half mile from the ship with nose high, out of wing-lift with no supplemental jet-lift, still approaching at seventy to eighty knots and started going down like a safe covered with owl shit.

Realizing my error, I powered up. However, I added power too late. The aircraft quickly dropped below the flight deck. I was able to stop the aircraft's forward motion by pulling back on the stick. Except unfortunately, the Harrier continued to descend toward the water.

I knew I was screwed, so I pushed the throttle through the limiters, which provided another nearly two thousand extra pounds of thrust. The additional thrust would provide increased vertical thrust. It was supposed to be done only when water injection was sprayed onto the turbine blades. The water injection would keep the engine from burning up due to the excessive RPM. But the Harrier I was flying had NO water on board to ingest! The aircraft was not only descending too fast but overheating the huge Pegasus engine, and in a matter of seconds the engine would become a molten mass!

I finally arrested the Harrier's sink rate. The aircraft was so close to the water the jet thrust was causing the ocean below to blow a white circle around the Harrier. I could see the red rotating beacon reflecting off the white spray all around the small jet fighter. What seemed like an eternity, but was in reality only seconds, passed, where I hung on expecting the Harrier to explode. I waited for the red, hot engine to impact the water, praying for the aircraft to climb, with me clinging on for dear life. I held true to the old fighter pilot adage, "*I would rather be dead than look bad!*" I continued to grasp the controls!

At the same time I could hear the landing signal officer in the tower of the *Guam* scream over the radio, "Eject! Eject!"

Ever so slowly the aircraft began to climb. Yes, and thank you, God! My aircraft continued to slowly ascend above the flight deck. The AV-8A lifted up and forward over the deck and I was able to make a safe, although rough, vertical landing. The fuel gauges were virtually on zero and the million-dollar Rolls-Royce Pegasus engine was a molten mass and would never fly again.

As I shut the aircraft down and opened the canopy, I felt the warm, summer breeze enter the cockpit and penetrate my flight suit. My flight suit was soaked with sweat from the sheer terror of the harrowing flight. I unstrapped, eager to exit my aircraft. I was shocked to discover I was unable to lift myself out of the cockpit. The medics arrived and took me to the ship's infirmary.

Fortunately my body recovered quickly. The doctor diagnosed my momentary paralysis as due to the terror of being so close to death for those long seconds I hovered near the water. My fear caused my body to pump so much adrenaline into my body that I was virtually poisoned. A good night's sleep in sick bay and a slight headache the next morning gave way to a quick recovery. I was soon returned to the flight schedule.

The experience was one of numerous flights in my navy flying career that caused me to realize pilots are a different breed. Carrier pilots spend many days of their lives being as close to death as one can come without achieving loss of life. The risks carrier pilots take aptly applies to many other areas of their lives, and not just when flying. The risks taken in our daily life are potentially destructive, such as on occasion consuming excessive amounts of alcohol, driving too fast, engaging in casual affairs and a reckless pursuit of self-gratification. Life is meant to be lived fully, but a look back would reveal a great deal of life outside of the cockpit would often turn out to be self-destructive.

"What a terrifying experience for you and your family." I said to Bud, "I am assuming you did share what happened to you with them." I looked at

Bud's expression and knew he had not told his wife or family and wondered why he hadn't.

He only laughed, "I think you care a little bit about me." Bud moved slowly toward me and without touching my lips I felt his caress. He took me in his arms and with the gentlest kiss changed the subject.

7
Bad Boys in Hack

THE RIDE ALONG PICTURESQUE HIGHWAY 1 overlooked the Pacific Ocean and was breathtaking, one we would recall with fond memories in the years ahead. I savored the personal pleasure of being with the man sitting beside me. We arrived in Monterey as the sun was setting over the horizon. The sun was a blazing burst of gold and in seconds disappeared from view. Monterey was California's first capital and offered some of the most historic and beautiful sites in the state. There were so many wonderful places for us to discover together.

While in Monterey we visited Fisherman's Wharf and enjoyed an early dinner at one of the local restaurants. After dinner we wandered around Cannery Row, where John Steinbeck drew inspiration for his novel, *Cannery Row*, about life in Monterey during the heyday of the sardine canning industry. I told Bud that John Steinbeck was one of my favorite authors. His book *The Grapes of Wrath* had inspired me to write about my early childhood.

We were charmed by the tranquil, quaint seaside town. Feeling carefree and adventuresome we took the time to enjoy the simple pleasure of an ice cream cone. I discovered it would always be a scoop of vanilla with hot fudge for Bud.

I tried a maple nut cone. We walked close together, contented to watch harbor seals, sea otters and pelicans in their natural waterfront environment.

Bud convinced me to spend the night, even though he could tell I thought staying overnight was crazy. I reminded him we hadn't made plans to stay and do what he wanted to do. He stroked and caressed me with tender kisses. "Live for the moment. Tonight may be a once in a lifetime opportunity!" I was caught up in the romantic atmosphere and I knew I wanted to spend more time alone with Bud. He convinced me by saying, "without a little spontaneity the world would be a dreary place, and we never know what tomorrow will bring."

The night was made for open windows, listening to the surf, the crash of waves and instinctive responses. Bud began another flying adventure before we fell asleep. He wanted to share more about his experiences flying the Harrier and his life with the VMA-513 Flying Nightmares. Before he began his story he added, "I pray you will not judge my bad boy behavior too harshly. I hope you will see beyond my wildness and even beyond the recklessness." He made sure we were both comfortable and passed a bottle of water to me and instead of his usual beer chose to have water as well.

I was on a lengthy detachment to China Lake with the Marine Harrier squadron, VMA-513 Flying Nightmares. China Lake was northeast of the Mojave Desert in Northwestern San Bernardino County, adjacent to Ridgecrest, California. The terrain varies from dry flat lake beds to rugged pinion pine-covered mountains. The majority of the land was undeveloped, sparsely populated, in a high desert area. It also has one of the largest wild horse populations in the United States. It is an excellent location for low-level flying, bombing and test flights. Several inventions including the AIM-9 Sidewinder, ACM-62 Walleye and AGM-45 Shrike had been developed, tested and refined in China Lake.

Soon after our squadron arrived in China Lake, the pilots bought several clunker cars for under a hundred dollars apiece. I couldn't remember whether we bothered with registration or license plates. When the training was completed and the squadron left China Lake to return to their home base in Beaufort, South Carolina, we took the clunkers out into the desert and played our version of demolition derby. The impromptu derby was great sport and we had fun running into one another until the cars were basically demolished.

Larry Wahl, my Navy contemporary, along with several Marine pilots, had been raging around all night and returned to our rooms at the Bachelor Officer Quarters sometime in the early hours of morning. If I noticed the yellow memo stickers on my door, I chose to ignore them and instead fell across my bed and into a deep sleep. I was awakened by the shrill ringing of the telephone on the nightstand beside my bed.

My wife Diane was calling to say I had been selected for promotion to Lieutenant Commander three years early! She asked, "Didn't you see the messages I had the Bachelor Officer Quarters front desk leave on your door?"

I opened the door to my room and saw at least a half dozen message stickers telling me to phone home. The messages would have been hard to miss had I not been drunk and chose to ignore them. "Sorry, Dee Dee," I said, "It was late when we finished flying. I crashed in Larry's room. I returned to my room a few minutes ago and picked up your messages and was getting ready to call just as you telephoned." If Diane thought my explanation odd, she didn't comment. I was sure she knew I was not being totally honest with her.

Early promotion was the exception in the Navy. A three-year early promotion was not only flattering but extremely humbling, in spite of the fact that the majority of aviators already thought highly of themselves. The Navy brass tended to keep their promotions right on schedule.

After hanging up the telephone I showered and shaved before stopping by the VMA-513 squadron office and hangar to see if anything interesting was happening. The squadron was standing down on Saturday to handle several maintenance gripes on aircraft. Larry was the scheduled duty officer for the squadron. He said, "I was lucky the activity in the squadron hanger was quiet when I took over duty and was able to get a few hours of sleep." Fortunately the squadron provided a cot for the officer on duty. I told Larry the good news about my promotion and added, "I'll hang around until you finish your watch and then let's head to the Officer's Club to celebrate."

As we entered the club I received several, "Well done, Squid. Cheers!" One beer led to more with me buying rounds and other officers joining the celebration as the evening progressed. Sometime after midnight Larry and I thought unscrewing the light bulbs in the bar chandelier would be hilarious. The chandelier was a large western wrought-iron wagon wheel with chains attached to the ceiling. Why we thought unscrewing light bulbs was a fun activity only someone with knowledge of the psychology of a naval aviator who is alcohol-impaired would understand. Anything goes!

There is one way families can better understand the psychology of a naval aviator related to the type of aircraft a pilot flew. The Navy explained the relationship by introducing the families to Captain Frank Dully.

Captain Frank Dully, a flight surgeon and Commanding Officer of the Naval Aviation Medical Institute, developed a theory of risk directly related to the type of aircraft a naval aviator flew. He would go aboard an aircraft carrier returning from cruise and give his brief to the Airwing before they returned home from cruise. He would later give a similar brief to the squadron wives in an effort to help them understand why their husbands were a different breed of men. Dr. Dully explained the changes the wives should expect when the men returned home after being away for six or more months.

The statistical data revealed that pilots typically are first born, the only male in the family or acted as the head of the family in some capacity. The same could be said for the women they would marry. The wives were first born, the only female or the female who was the caregiver of the family. He equated relative risk to the type of aircraft pilots flew and the degree of risk taking and daring they were likely to exhibit both in and outside of the cockpit. The hierarchy showed the Harrier as the highest risk and most difficult to fly. Other high-risk aircraft included the Navy F-8 Crusader, F-4 Phantom and the F-14 Tomcat fighters. Also included were the light attack aircraft, A-4 Skyhawks, A-7 Corsairs and helicopters.

There was no question that in 1973 a Harrier pilot flying the AV-8A with its Rolls-Royce Pegasus engine would find he was close to death without achieving the end of his natural life on a regular basis. The same was not true for other aircraft flown by naval aviators. Some would say Harrier pilots were courageous. Some would say they were crazy. However one characterized the men who flew the AV-8A Harrier, they took the greatest risk!

So back inside the Officer's Club the boys were about to cross the line. I never blamed my wildness or rowdiness on alcohol. Larry and I just thought unscrewing the lightbulbs and pouring beer into the empty light sockets was hilarious. On the third light bulb socket the fixture blew up, knocking us on our asses and concurrently blowing out the power in the Officer's Club.

Somehow when Larry and I could no longer remain in a steady upright position we stumbled out of the club, much too intoxicated to drive our De Soto clunker, and walked back to the BOQ.

The next morning Major Bob O'Dare was pounding on my door. Major O'Dare epitomized the consummate Marine image. He was the ideal persona of a handsome Marine aviator, and resembled the late actor Steve McQueen. Among his skills, Major O'Dare had the ability to glance at a woman and know her bra size. If he got close enough he could even tell what fragrance she was wearing. I thought Bob's skill an amazing talent and one worth achieving. I loved being around women but never reached Bob's level of expertise.

Major O'Dare woke me up by continuing to pound on my door and then left to wake Larry. He snapped, "Skipper Baker wants to see you both in the ready room within the hour so get your butts out of bed."

Skipper Baker had received a call from the base Commanding Officer (CO) informing him about Larry's and my escapade at the Officer's Club. Fortunately, this was not the CO's first encounter with the antics of rowdy aviators and he appeared to empathize with their unorthodox celebrations. The Commanding Officer and Skipper Baker were both aviators and responsive to reasons given when celebrations got out of hand. On many occasions the wildly playful or funny actions were a release from an accident or even the loss of a colleague and occasionally the stunts were simply a way of letting off steam.

Skipper Baker promised the CO of the base he would put the boys in hack. They were in trouble and the Skipper would administer some type of punishment. Larry and I were taken off the flight schedule and later the same afternoon driven by a Navy driver out into the desert to a target range called the Ponderosa. We were to observe the bombing practice of a division of Harriers dropping live napalm.

We were so hung over that every move we made was painful. We each prayed for a nap to sleep off the aftereffects of too much fun. It was well over a hundred degrees outside and the desert cactus and flora was much more dense and taller than the plants looked from the air. We stumbled through the sage brush and sand in what we thought was the correct direction.

Suddenly Larry and I found ourselves in a clearing with large rings on it. "Holy crap," we exclaimed, "we're on the fucking target!"

Larry and I looked up as we heard four Harriers screaming toward us in formation at two hundred feet above the ground. "What the fuck," Larry yelled, "they're flying right toward us. Are we even at the right observation site?"

The four Harriers continued toward us. I could see two large silver canisters the size of shiny beer kegs filled with napalm under the wings of each Harrier! The Harriers buzzed us as we ran for cover. It was a futile attempt to get away from the Harriers carrying the napalm canisters. Larry and I continued to run, terrified we were standing where the Harriers planned to drop their fire bombs.

Running was a useless effort to try and outrun aircraft flying at five hundred knots and two hundred feet off the ground. Larry and I ran as fast as we could, falling face down in the desert sand in an attempt to put distance between ourselves and our would-be attackers. We realized the Marine pilots were laughing at us as they banked hard left and flew on to the actual target. Larry and I finally relaxed. We sat down exhausted as we watched the fire and flash of the napalm bombing runs several miles away.

Bud seemed afraid to look at me as he finished the story. He glanced over and said, "This is the first time I can't read your expression, let alone guess what you're thinking." However, I can hear my Censor screaming, *"Well if you wanted to paint a negative picture of your outrageous and self-destructive exploits you just did a damn good job."*

"Fran, I hate too much silence. It is almost as terrifying as seeing a red light in the cockpit." Silence hovered in the room until Bud asked, "Are you sorry I told you the story?"

I needed to give myself a moment before I answered Bud's question, "Since the night we met I have been trying to grasp what separates you the man from you the naval aviator. When you were on exchange duty with the Marines and flew the Harrier it sounded like that was who you were, all you were. I don't think you allowed room for the exceptional man within you to exist. I can understand the risk you took to become the first Navy pilot to fly the Harrier in fleet operations. I can also grasp your wanting to be the best LSO in the Navy and how being a carrier pilot distinguishes you and sets you apart from other professionals. However, I can't comprehend the risk and recklessness you took which eventually jeopardized your marriage. Being a carrier pilot defines you and perhaps you would not be the man you are becoming without the experiences of the past. My heart aches that you wasted so many days and nights. I have sympathy for the woman whose happiness was compromised because of your behavior. If you needed to sow your wild oats, I would say you did more than your share."

"Well she didn't say she wanted to leave and never see you again, so I guess there may be hope for you yet," said my Censor. "You have been in tough spots before and survived. Tell her about the beauty and majesty of flying over the polar ice cap."

8
Polar Opposites

"Fran, I took a risk and exposed a self-destructive side of my personality. But there is so much more I want share with you. Wherever I fly I am exposed to rare sights that can only be seen from the air. I sit all alone in my cockpit with no one to share or describe what it is I am privileged to witness."

Such was the time in 1973 when I deployed on the *USS Guam* with a detachment from VMA-513 Flying Nightmares. We had four AV-8A Harriers, six pilots and associated maintenance personnel aboard. We headed to the freezing North Atlantic with Major Bud Isles as the detachment commander. I was second in command of the sea control detachment.

The mission of our small force was twofold. We had onboard the *Guam* a Navy SH-3 Sea King helicopter in addition to the four Harriers. The SH-3 Sea King was modified with a retractable dome in the belly of the helicopter. We were not privy to the mission of the dome as shipboard personnel ran the classified part of the test program.

Also aboard the *Guam* were two Lamps Mark I helicopters to fly rescue combat air patrol for the Harriers. In addition to rescue air patrol the helicopters flew anti-submarine warfare missions, assisting the Coast Guard cutter in the small task force. The Harrier squadron was gathering data on the AV-8A's performance in cold weather operations as a part of the task force's mission.

Strange as it would seem today, there was no satellite equipment aboard any of the ships who could accurately tell how close we were to the polar ice cap. One very exciting, memorable mission I flew was with Captain Jewt Collier as my wingman. We launched before dawn and our mission was to locate the ever-moving polar ice cap.

Jewt and I flew for about forty minutes or three hundred miles at fifteen thousand feet. Just as the sun was rising we witnessed the most spectacular sunrise imaginable. The sun poked its head up over the magnificent polar ice cap. This seemingly endless sheet of beautiful white ice looked like a giant jigsaw puzzle from the air. Jewt and I could see cracks where the ice cap had broken up and shifted back together as it migrated across the North Atlantic Ocean. The amazing view was a sight few human beings have ever seen. The sensational vista before me was one I will never forget.

On returning from our mission, and almost back to the ship, I spotted a giant iceberg floating about ten miles from the *USS Guam*. I pointed down with hand signals, indicating to Jewt for us to descend and take a closer look. Jewt and I rolled in a section formation, as if we had spotted a target and were on a bombing run. I signaled for Jewt to drop back into a tail chase formation. As our aircraft approached the giant cube of ice, we decelerated and lowered our nozzles in order to hover around the iceberg.

I was amazed at the majesty and beauty surrounding us. Rather than the iceberg being one solid block of ice, it appeared to be an upside-down tricuspid tooth, with the roots extending high into the air for at least two hundred feet. The iceberg rocked gently to and fro as we circled slowly around it. Jewt and I flew closer to the incredible sight and saw a pool of water trapped in the center of the iceberg. The pool was gently shifting as the iceberg continued to rock to and fro. The water was crystal clear and was the most radiant turquoise blue I had ever seen. I maneuvered away from the iceberg to allow Jewt to fly his Harrier closer in order to take a photograph with the sixty millimeter reconnaissance camera in my aircraft. I kept the photo and although it was in black and white, the image continues to hold the splendor and grandeur of a very unique moment in time. To watch a Harrier with its nozzles down hovering right next to one of God's magnificent creations was truly a once in a lifetime experience. I witnessed an ethereal vision that very few human beings have ever seen and certainly none from the cockpit of a small fighter jet.

Jewt and I were shocked out of our tranquil moment and almost out of fuel when we received a harsh call from the Air Boss aboard the USS *Guam* instructing us to land immediately!

We landed back aboard the ship where the weather had begun to deteriorate. Our small carrier, *Guam*, was in range of Russian Bear aircraft and had received orders not to allow the Russian pilots to fly their aircraft within fifty nautical miles of the small task force. A Harrier would quickly be launched to escort the Russian Bear and ensure the foreign aircraft kept its distance. Exercises such as we participated in were part of naval aviation's role in bringing the Cold War to a close as we demonstrated to the Soviets that we could strike and destroy their vital strategic assets with carrier-based air power.

The next day was stormy with rain and sleet splattering down on the flight deck. I was in launch position, strapped into a Harrier which was tied down on the very stern of the ship. The AV-8A generator was running to provide electrical power and radio contact to the tower in the event the Harrier had to be launched, intercept and escort a Russian Bear away from the task force.

One of the small Lamps helicopters was on the bow of the *Guam* with its engines running and the rotor blades engaged, preparing for take-off on an anti-submarine mission. The *Guam* was crashing into the sea with green water pouring over the bow and white water spraying all the way up to the bridge. The ship took a heavy roll to starboard, and it looked as if the helicopter would slide off the deck. In the Air Operations, the Air Boss must have also thought the helicopter would do that because he radioed with a great sense of urgency to the pilot, "Spartan 03, you are cleared to lift off!" The Air Boss wanted the helicopter to get airborne before it slid any farther toward the starboard side of the ship. The pilot quickly lifted off the flight deck. Then all HELL broke loose.

I had been in this situation before, sitting by myself in the cockpit of a small jet fighter. My Harrier was on the stern of the ship, facing the bow. I watched the ship cast about with over forty knots of wind. The scene before me appeared in black and white. I could see the driving rain blowing sleet and water spray over the bow and down the flight deck. All of a sudden my view toward the bow was blurred. The only thing I could observe was a cloud of black objects flying toward me as I sat inside the cockpit of the Harrier. I felt a THUD down near my nose wheel with objects continuing to blow past the cockpit. It was impossible for me to see or know what was happening below my aircraft.

As debris blew past the Harrier, I could see the Lamps Mark I helicopter on the bow, spinning on its side in a circle. One of the main mounts appeared to be still attached to the flight deck, causing the aircraft to continue to whirl. The helicopter was tethered to the deck by the left tie down chain. When the spinning stopped, the pilot secured the engines and the crew inside the helicopter evacuated what was left of the Lamps Mark I uninjured.

I was positive I would not be launched any time soon due to the helicopter accident and debris on the flight deck. I quickly unstrapped and started climbing down the ladder to the deck. The wind and sea spray were clouding my vision but I could see flight deck personnel running toward the Harrier. A few airmen crowded under the nose wheel of the aircraft as I jumped the final step down to the flight deck. To my shock and horror, I saw what the thump I had felt was while sitting inside the Harrier.

As the helicopter attempted to lift off with the tie down chain still attached to the left main mount, the aircraft rolled onto its portside. The nearly supersonic fiberglass rotor blades immediately impacted the steel flight deck. The rotor blades disintegrated into a cloud of dense pieces and had been hurled down the flight deck by the high winds. The rotor blade pieces flew toward my aircraft. A yellow shirt had been standing about twelve feet in front of the nose of the Harrier. He had been hit by a large piece of rotor blade and thrown against the nose wheel of my aircraft. The THUD I heard was that of the body of an eighteen-year-old airman, serving his country overseas. The young airman was performing a difficult job in dangerous conditions and had been killed by the impact of a rotor blade slamming him into the nose wheel of my Harrier.

The *USS Guam* was the largest ship in the task force and due to our location in the Atlantic had no access to land. Therefore, the task force had no way to immediately transport the body of the airman stateside. The medics placed his body in a large refrigerator aboard the ship until the *Guam* finished her mission and returned to the coast of North Carolina. From North Carolina the body of the young airman was flown to his home port in Norfolk for a private burial. To this brave young man, "Fair winds and following seas."

I finished my story aware I had talked more about myself to Fran than any woman I had known and momentarily imagined what it would be like to have this woman waiting for me when I came home from flying. The thought of being in Fran's welcoming arms every night and going to sleep with a smile on my face was worth the lecture from my Censor.

Before my Censor could say a word, I said, "I know, I know, it's too soon. I'm not ready for this! But, I can dream, can't I? This smart, sexy, beautiful woman likes me and I don't have to hide anything from her. In fact, she finds me irresistible, so leave me alone!"

Since we were having such a good time I suggested we drive to San Francisco and spend the night. While we were there I wanted to tell Fran why I volunteered to leave my Navy squadron and favorite Commanding Officer. I wanted to tell her my goal to be the first naval aviator to fly the Harrier with **the few, the proud, the Marines** in fleet operations.

9
The Death Machine

I AGREED TO GO TO SAN Francisco, the beautiful city on the bay, on one condition. Bud promised we would go shopping after checking into our hotel near Fisherman's Wharf. Bud seemed perfectly comfortable in what he was wearing but I was tired of wearing the same clothing for two days.

He said, "What the heck, it is the least I can do for you. I'll even tag along and carry your bags."

Bud thought shopping meant I only wanted to buy something new just for myself. I had other plans for the afternoon. Before the day was over Bud had a new suit, shirt and a pair of the popular Frye boots. My treat! I tried to be subtle and not critical of what he had worn on our date. But I really didn't care for polyester! I asked Bud to touch the fabrics of the clothing I thought would look attractive on him and see if he could feel the difference.

He smiled. "Beautiful lady, you have such class. I'm willing to learn. I remember our first night together and how I liked touching the fabric of what you were wearing. I was unfamiliar with how rich a fabric can feel."

Bud felt the need to add, "Of course, I loved touching you so much more."

We enjoyed an early dinner at Fisherman's Wharf, savoring a Crab Louie salad and bottle of chardonnay. The restaurant had panoramic windows and Bud mentioned he could tell I was enjoying being near the water. He said, "Your green eyes sparkle as you watch the ships and boats pass under the Golden Gate Bridge."

After dinner we walked to our hotel and Bud suggested he tell another Harrier story. He had already shared how unstable and dangerous the Harrier was to fly. I said, "You are much more complex and willing to take risks than I had first thought. From what you have already told me I see the effect the tour with the Marines has had on your life. If I remember correctly, in 1972 you were twenty-nine-years old, a Navy Lieutenant, a flight instructor and the senior landing signal officer in the Replacement Air Group. Why did you change directions in your career plans?"

Before I answered Fran I made sure she was comfortable. "One afternoon as I was completing required paperwork I received a life-changing telephone call from my former Commanding Officer, Captain Bob Thomas. Captain Thomas had been my Skipper when I served with VA-113 Stingers during combat aboard the *USS Enterprise*."

Captain Thomas was working in the Pentagon for the Chief of Naval Operations (CNO) and the United States Marine Corps AV-8A Harrier was one of his programs. The Admiral Elmo Zumwalt, the CNO, intended to select a U.S. Navy pilot to go on exchange duty with the first operational Marine Harrier squadron. The Navy exchange pilot would report back directly to him on matters related to shipboard compatibility of the British Hawker Siddley AV-8A Harrier. Captain Thomas wanted to throw my name into the ring.

"I'm flattered. Let me think about the offer and I'll get back to you as soon as possible," I replied.

The next day I made an appointment with my current Commanding Officer, Captain John (Nick) Nicholson. Captain Nick had a rare combination of talents. He was my mentor, an exceptional leader I deeply admired and respected. The Skipper was a short, stocky man, a boisterous voice and was a conduit of energy.

The Death Machine

After explaining the proposed Harrier program to Captain Nick he exploded, "Why in the hell would you want to do a damn thing like that? You have a great career ahead of you, but first you need to fill all the right blocks. You had a good combat tour. You didn't get your ass shot off. Thank the Lord!"

On my first combat tour during the Vietnam War, I was a greenhorn. Skipper Nick was the Executive Officer with VA-56 Champs, aboard the *USS Enterprise*. My squadron VA-113 Stingers was the sister squadron to the Champs. During the cruise I became acquainted with him and often relied on his good counsel and trusted his guidance.

"Bud," Captain Nick said, "You are my best LSO and I want you to finish your job with the Flying Eagles. Then take a good sea duty assignment. After that you will be promoted to Lieutenant Commander and ready for your department head tour. With this career path you are destined to screen for command of an A-7 Corsair II squadron. Why in the hell would you want to go fly some goofy British jet with the *Jarheads*? By the time you return to the fleet no one will know who you are!"

Captain Nick was a scary guy when he screamed and cursed. I listened, took my scolding and quietly left his office.

After a couple of days thinking about what I wanted to do, I was ready to give Captain Nick my decision. I walked into his office, stood with my head high, shoulders back and said, "Skipper, I have decided I want to fly the Harrier with the Marines."

Captain Nick stood up and walked across his big office. The same office I would occupy years later when I commanded VA-122 Flying Eagles. He shook my hand and gave me a big bear hug and said, "Buddy, be the best damn Harrier pilot the Marines have ever seen. Good luck!"

Fran interrupted, "Why was flying with the Marines so important? Why were you so eager to make such a major change in your life?"

"Hell, Fran, I didn't really think about it. To me a Marine was the poster child of bravery and courage. I grew to manhood imagining a swaggering self-confident masculine ideal that I wanted to become. Now was my chance and it was a risk I needed to take."

"Why didn't you just join the Marines if they were your ideal?"

"Good question. I did consider joining. However, I needed a guarantee that I would fly jets and become a carrier pilot. By taking this exchange tour with the Marines I would become a Harrier pilot and have the best of both worlds."

I went on telling Fran that I ran out of the Captain Nick's office and the squadron hangar exhilarated. I took a deep breath of air and yelled, "Hot damn!" I called Captain Thomas and said, "I'm in!"

Within a month, the selection was made from the list of nominees and I was thrilled to be selected. The orders arrived a week later and said I was to report to the Commanding Officer of VMA-513 Flying Nightmares, at Marine Corps Air Station, Beaufort, South Carolina, for duties involving flying. Before going to Beaufort I would temporarily train at Naval Air Station Patuxent River, Maryland."

The Flying Nightmares Detachment Alfa had a small detachment of Marines at the Navy Test Pilot Center in Patuxent River. Patuxent River Naval Air Station is located at the mouth of the Patuxent River in beautiful southern Maryland and has one of the most vital shoreline installations in existence today.

When I arrived at Patuxent River Naval Air Station there were three Harriers undergoing acceptance and weapons testing being flown by five Marine officers, all graduates of the Navy Test Pilot School. The Marine Corps was aware of the inherent stability problems of the Harrier, and did not want them highlighted through navy testing. As previously mentioned, the Marine Corps was successful in convincing the Armed Services Committee to accept the purchase of the Harrier because the British were flying the aircraft operationally. The acquisition was an *off the shelf* buy. The Marine Corps further explained to the Armed Services Committee the Marine test pilots would do their own testing due to their orientation toward the Marine Corps mission.

Things were extremely hectic the day I checked into the Quonset hut where Detachment Alfa was administered. Major Mike Ripley, one of the five test pilots, had been flying a Harrier on a routine test hop. He was firing rockets at an instrumented target in the water off the coast of the Naval Air Station. The heads-up display (HUD) in the Harrier had the capability of capturing video of what the pilot was seeing in real time. On most test ranges telemetry cameras capture the entire evolution so there would be no question about the sequence of events.

On Major Ripley's third rocket run he stayed in the dive longer than normal in an effort to capture his own rocket hits on the HUD camera film. Regrettably, the extended dive took him out of the envelope to recover. His aircraft was descending with the nose high when it impacted the water and blew up. Unfortunately, he did not survive the crash.

Fran stopped me as tears welled up in her eyes, "How horrible, and on your first day of reporting for duty. Did you think about changing your mind about flying the Harrier?"

"Franny, it certainly was unsettling and I was off to a sad beginning on my first day reporting for duty. But no, his death didn't change my mind. I wanted the opportunity to fly the Harrier. The Marines not only had lost Major Ripley, a valued test pilot, but also one of the only three Harriers in the country."

The next morning I met with Major Bud Isles, a seasoned test pilot who had accumulated many hours flying the Harrier with the British in England. He was the Operations Officer and my new boss. He would turn out to be the ideal instructor to train new pilots to fly the Harrier. As we met in the lobby of the Bachelor Officer Quarters, Major Isles approached me with a cool look and said, "Are you Orr?" I replied in the affirmative, noting this was the first and only time I had been approached by another officer by my last name. In the Navy the last name was only used when you addressed an enlisted person.

Major Isles and I walked from the Bachelor Officer Quarters to the Quonset hut where Detachment Alfa had their morning briefings. We sat in the middle of forty folding chairs, on a highly polished and spotless concrete floor. The chairs were mostly filled, and there was a buzz of conversation among the Marines, both officer and enlisted personnel. The conversations centered on Major Ripley's fatal accident the previous day.

At exactly 0730 the room became totally silent. I cautiously looked over my shoulder to see what was happening. I could not see anything but heard an unusual *click-click, click-click*. The source of the clicking was a small, impeccably groomed man in Marine greens. Everything on his body was shining, from his shoes to his gold naval aviator wings and medals. Yes, even his head was shining, with a closely cropped haircut framing his face. His face was deeply tanned and chiseled with high cheekbones often seen on a person of American Indian descent. As this impeccable Marine walked crisply down the aisle, I could see the *click-click* was coming from the taps on his black shoes, and was the only sound in the room. I whispered to Major Isles, "Who the fuck is that?" To which Major Isles replied with a sinister grin, "He's your new boss!"

The Marines did not allow the unfortunate accident and death of Major Ripley to alter their schedule, and pressed on with training for carrier qualification. Although I had not flown the Harrier, one of the primary criteria for my selection to Marine exchange duty was to be a landing signal officer. I was not only an experienced landing signal officer but a damn good one!

After being briefed by the test pilots on the unique approach and landing procedures of the Harrier, the detachment started field carrier landing practice (FCLP) for the next several weeks. We were scheduled for landing qualification on two U.S. Navy Amphibious assault ships; the *USS Guadalcanal*, a landing platform helicopter ship, and the *USS Coronado*, a landing platform deck ship, a much smaller ship with only a helicopter landing area on the stern.

The test pilots were highly skilled aviators with instinctive judgment and had previously carrier qualified in conventional aircraft in the Navy training command. They were familiar with what a landing signal officer's role was in assisting pilots to land aboard an aircraft carrier. Just as in the Navy, the landing signal officer's primary responsibility was to project a calm voice, convey confidence and coach a pilot making a difficult landing aboard the aircraft carrier. The test pilots had also trained in the Harrier in the United Kingdom and were very capable and quick to learn and respond to LSO calls for line up and power. The tests on both the *Guadalcanal* and *Coronado* were highly successful and without incident.

I completed temporary duty at Patuxent River and was excited to be on my way to the Marine Corps Air Station in Beaufort, South Carolina and my turn to fly the Harrier. "Fran, have you been to Beaufort?" I asked.

"No," she said.

"Beaufort is located on Port Royal Island and is the second oldest city in South Carolina. It is renowned for its scenic location and also for maintaining a historic character through the city's impressive antebellum architecture. It is the home to the Marine Corps Air Station Beaufort and is adjacent to the Marine Corps Parris Island, and the Beaufort Naval Hospital. Before leaving

Beaufort in 1973 for my next duty station my son Shane was born at the Naval Hospital."

On my first day at the squadron in Beaufort I was met by Captain Toby Griggs. Captain Griggs, the Commanding Officer, Lieutenant Colonel (Bud) Baker and the Sergeant Major were the only three members of the squadron other than the maintenance crew in the hangar across the street.

Toby was excited to have a contemporary in the squadron and greeted me warmly. He said, "First, you need to call on the Sergeant Major, and then the Commanding Officer, Lieutenant Colonel (Bud) Baker." In 1972 the Navy had no senior enlisted equivalent to a Sergeant Major. I was not sure why I needed to call on an *enlisted man*. However, I took Captain Griggs suggestion. I learned very quickly that being a Sergeant Major was a highly revered position. As I followed Toby into the Sergeant Major's spacious and spotless office I saw a handsome, middle-aged gentleman sitting at his desk, hands folded one on top of the other. Behind him was an American flag flanking one side of his desk and the U.S. Marine Corps flag on the other.

As we approached the Sergeant Major he stood behind his desk and offered a strong and welcoming handshake. After Toby introduced me, the Sergeant Major said, "Please have a seat, Lieutenant." Immediately, Captain Griggs departed the room and quietly closed the door behind him. There was an eerie sense of maturity and command in this handsome noncommissioned Marine. He politely asked about my previous flying experience, my family and my aspirations. When we were finished with the pleasantries, the Sergeant Major leaned forward in his seat, and loomed over his large desk. He was physically close and softly said to me, "Well, Lieutenant, VMA-513 is going to be a great tour for you. But first, you need to cut your sideburns and hair, and second you need to run with us."

These were the Zumwalt days. Admiral Elmo Zumwalt had been nominated by President Richard Nixon to be the Chief of Naval Operations in 1970. The Admiral was a ship driver (not an aviator) and well-known for his long black hair and huge pork chop sideburns. When he took command of the Navy, the CNO revolutionized the grooming standards that had been in place for decades. He approved longer hair and neat facial hair. Beards and mustaches were allowed for all ranks, and sideburns could be worn down to the bottom of the ears. The Admiral made the move in an effort to reduce racism and sexism within the Navy, which had been on the rise.

I realized I must have looked like someone out of a rock band to the Sergeant Major, compared to my Marine contemporaries who were so *high and tight*. A bit taken back by his remarks, I sat up straight and tall saying, "I will do both, Sergeant Major." I did, and the Sergeant Major and I became good friends as he continued to mentor me in the ways of the Marine Corps.

My next meeting was with the Skipper of VMA-513, Lieutenant Colonel Bud Baker. Colonel Baker was also an impressive man, suntanned and athletic, although he seemed a bit old to me. I thought he was at least forty years old. He welcomed me to the Flying Nightmares and wished me a good tour with the Corps.

At the time I checked in, none of the Harriers had been delivered to the squadron from the United Kingdom. In order for the pilots to maintain currency in flight operations, the squadron flew in the two-seat TA-4F Skyhawks. When all of the new pilots finally checked into the squadron we detached to the Marine Corps Air Station, New River helicopter base in Jacksonville, North Carolina, for helicopter training.

Since the Marine Corps chose not to purchase the two-seat trainer variant of the Harrier, there was no way to train for vertical take-off, landings and transitional flight. Instead, vertical training was done by the VMA-513 pilots flying helicopters. The CH-46 Sea Knight helicopter built by Boeing Vertol was the aircraft of choice for our type of training and another good decision the Marine Corps made.

The reason for choosing the CH-46 was because it was very stable to fly when the stability augmentation systems (SAS) was on. With the SAS off the helicopter flew much like the Harrier. The CH-46 had the same vulnerable traits as the Harrier in transitional flight with negative stability in all three axes, with a proclivity to fly upside down and backwards. The sensitive axes of the CH-46 was particularly good training for the prospective Harrier pilots. A change in axis could quickly put the aircraft out of control and in an ejection situation for the pilot.

The ten of us qualified in day and night landings on small helicopter pads surrounding the Air Station. One cloudy, starless night I was flying a CH-46 Sea Knight helicopter. A Marine Captain flight instructor from the

The Death Machine

training squadron was in the left seat, with a single Marine crewman in the back. I was making an approach to a sparsely lit one hundred-square-foot pad. I decelerated the helicopter by easing the stick back. I fought the heavy rudder controls and eased the nose higher to decelerate as I struggled to keep the small pad in sight. I lowered the nose as my airspeed depleted to *air taxi* into a hover. Just as I was getting comfortable and about fifty feet above the pad, the aft tunnel of the aircraft lit up behind me with a flash and loud explosion. KABOOM!

The Captain, who had hundreds of hours flying the CH-46 helicopter, quickly said, "I've got it" and took over the controls. He had recognized my inexperience at having less than five hours in flying a helicopter and recognized a genuine emergency of landing the aircraft on one engine. He expertly and skillfully lowered the Sea Knight down to the pad for a safe single-engine landing. He disengaged the rotor while the crewman jumped out to secure the CH-46 and survey the damage.

The left engine had suffered catastrophic foreign object damage. The engine literally ate itself by ingesting something from the landing pad into the engine. The pilot radioed back to the training squadron ready room for a replacement helicopter to be sent immediately. When it arrived the Captain, crewman and I jumped inside the new helicopter and took off to finish training for the night. The damaged bird was left stranded on the pad to be recovered the next day.

After completing helicopter training each pilot had one last test to pass before his first flight in the AV-8A Harrier. In order to graduate we needed to demonstrate our newly learned skill of flying day and night in the vertical to the Executive Officer, Major Bill Scheuren. Everyone in the class had been well trained and passed, allowing the exciting transition of flying the Harrier to begin.

The primary reason for the success of the first Harrier pilots trained in the United States was the exceptional, thorough, and regimented ground school course on STOVL Aerodynamics taught by Operations Officer Major Bud Isles. He was pragmatic, analytical and a smart test pilot who had many hours in the AV-8A Harrier. He had flown the Harrier extensively with the Brits in the United Kingdom. Major Isles, more than anyone else, knew and acknowledged the inherent dangers that came with flying this unusual aircraft.

He explained why these dangers existed, and precisely what a pilot needed to know about the aerodynamics of the Harrier in order to stay alive.

The first two training flights were straight conventional flying or taking off and landing like a normal jet without using the nozzles. The wing was so small that take-off speed with full internal fuel was right at one hundred and eighty knots or two hundred and eight miles per hour. Maximum speed on the runway was limited by the rotation speed of the small outrigger wheels that could only go one hundred and eighty knots before exploding. When you landed the aircraft conventionally at one hundred and sixty-five or one hundred and ninety miles per hour the Harrier was dangerous. The danger was not just from the speed but also the aircraft became very *squirrely* at high speed on the ground. In order to stop the aircraft before running out of runway I would select the braking stop on the nozzle handle, then power was added to the engine to gain the advantage of reverse thrust from the engine before I slowed down to braking speed.

Although conventional landings were difficult and dangerous in the Harrier, it was appropriate to start the syllabus with something with which we were familiar. In three years I never made another conventional landing in the Harrier because it was considered an emergency procedure.

The second of the three stages of training was straight vertical take-off and landings. The aircraft would be light loaded with fuel to allow vertical take-off for the given temperatures. The day we did our first vertical flight was memorable as vertical take-off was the first utilization of the STOVL capabilities of the aircraft. STOVL capabilities distinguished the Harrier pilots from all other jet pilots. It was also an exciting day with Lieutenant General George Axtell, Commanding General of the First Marine Airwing, and his Deputy Brigadier General Tom Miller (known as the *father of the Harrier* in the U.S. Marine Corps) in attendance. Both generals, along with Lieutenant Colonel Bud Baker, sat in folding chairs on the end of the runway observing each of the ten pilots as we made our first vertical take-off and landing.

The last stage of the familiarization training was the most complex and dangerous. A short take-off and landing was the most challenging. I was required to transition through the daunting thirty- to ninety-knot range during which the aircraft was negatively stable in all three axes.

When ready for take-off, the pilot would release the brakes, then push the throttle to full power, which energized the nearly twenty thousand pounds of thrust from the Rolls-Royce Pegasus engine and very rapidly propelled the small jet forward. At sixty knots or approximately seventy miles per hour the pilot would rotate the nozzle control handle to a stop that was set at sixty degrees. The aircraft would literally jump off the runway, at which time the Harrier was flying semi-jet borne, meaning that the Harrier was utilizing partial wing-lift and partial jet-borne lift. As the pilot very gently moved the nozzle handle forward the actual nozzles move aft to a lesser degree of rotation. The resulting aft thrust was translated quickly into wing-lift. The faster the aircraft was flying the more quickly the pilot could move the nozzle handle forward and capture more wing-lift at a higher rate.

In a normal transition the pilot would be airborne with sixty degrees of nozzles and full power. He would move the nozzle handle forward at a smooth rate to maximize acceleration forward while simultaneously achieving the desired rate of climb away from the runway.

When the Harrier was designed and built in England the AV-8A was not sophisticated enough to compensate for the innate aerodynamic shortcomings of the aircraft. This is what made the Harrier so dangerous and challenging to fly. However, my squadron lost only one airplane in over three years of flying, and that accident was due to a bird strike.

Fran said, "It seems the U.S. Marine Corps made an excellent decision at the very beginning of the Harrier program."

She is right. The theory was that it was easier to teach a jet pilot to hover than teach a helicopter pilot to fly a conventional aircraft. History proved the Marine Corps theory true. Our outstanding safety record as the first operational Harrier squadron in the United States was because of the background of the first pilots Major Bud Isles trained.

In the late 1970s the Marines changed course and put helicopter pilots and brand new pilots right out of the training command into the AV-8A. The helicopter pilots, along with the less experienced pilots, crashed Harriers all over the countryside. The AV-8A was then dubbed the *Death Machine*! Eleven years after Major Isle's initial and exemplary training the Marine Corps AV-8A Harrier accrued an appalling record with the loss of some fifty-five aircraft in peacetime accidents. The appalling record meant that eight years after Major

Isles left the VMA-513 Flying Nightmares the Marine Corps lost an average of seven Harriers per year. Based on the accident record in the United States as well as other countries which flew the AV-8A, Harrier was regarded as *one of the most dangerous aircraft in the world to fly.*

I listened as Bud finished his story and was a bit overwhelmed by the aerodynamic tutorial. After hearing the final chapter of his Harrier tour I had several questions I wanted to ask him. Was he always willing to take risks? What about the exploits he was involved in? He cheated on his wife. Was that his past and now he wanted to change? By giving him my heart would I find myself walking a similar path of his ex-wife? If I focused on the danger of flying would it affect our relationship in the future?

For tonight I allowed Bud to think whatever he wanted as I sorted through my feelings toward him. Besides, I was carrying around a secret and before much longer would need to share it with him. That might make my questions unnecessary. I wish I had a Navy wife to talk to and get her thoughts on what she feels about her husband putting on his flight suit, knowing he could walk into harm's way.

Before meeting Bud I had no idea what a Harrier looked like. I had seen the pictures of him standing beside the aircraft or with his squadron. I had thought he looked sexy and masculine, even cocky and arrogant. Not once did I associate Bud with being in danger flying the Harrier. Now I would never be able to look at it in the same way.

I had to admit our world was one of polar opposites. I wasn't brave and I've never felt the need to be adventuresome. I try to be cautious in my view of life. Looking at how I have behaved with Bud is a contradiction of who I am or who I think I am. Then again, when he looks at me with his luminous blue eyes and smiles my heart is captured and I am ready to join the next adventure with him.

10
The Woman Worth Pursuing

The following evening Bud and I attended a squadron party at the Commanding Officer's home. As we joined the party I lifted my eyes and was captured by the warmth and undeniable desire twinkling in his eyes. He looked at me as if no woman interested him in the slightest as we walked in together.

During the party a couple of the wives cornered me and asked about the amount of time I had been spending with Bud. I blushed in response to their curiosity but wasn't offended. I answered them by saying, "I believe Bud is one of the most eligible bachelors on the base and certainly seems to be the Warhawks' favorite."

The wives agreed. One said, "He is a charming flirt, quick to pass out compliments and is wild in ways we wouldn't want our husbands to behave. Bud is always fun at a party and a good dancer. He has assured us on more than one occasion, should one of us find ourselves single, we would become a *target of opportunity*. Of course, we think he was probably kidding."

I had no problem with the wives seeing happiness glowing in my eyes. I assumed the Navy wives questioning me had experienced a similar phenomenon when they found themselves wrapped in a cocoon of love with their naval aviator. I smiled and said, "I find myself captivated and overwhelmed by Bud's natural exuberance, his passion for flying and the danger all aviators risk daily. However, it is the man, his incredible daring, energy and flaws which fascinate me and make him so interesting. Frankly I am stunned at the depth of my caring for a man I have known for such a short period of time."

I paused searching for the next word and spoke as one looking through the eyes of love, "I'm not sure what the future holds, because I must return to Virginia. A long-distance relationship with Bud will be difficult and most likely impossible to sustain."

On the way to Bud's apartment after the party, I told him I would be returning to Virginia Beach the next day. Bud seemed jolted by the news that I would be leaving Lemoore so soon. Unashamed of the moisture in his eyes, he pleaded for me to stay a few more days.

"I'm so sorry, as much as I wish that was possible I have responsibilities and must return home," I sighed. "We can write one another."

The next morning we drove under threatening skies to the Fresno Airport. Bud was as turbulent as the weather and pulled over to the side of the road before we reached the airport entrance. "Fran," he implored, "I care for you. I can't predict the future but I know I want you to stay a few more days."

I looked quietly into his moist blue eyes, deeply moved by his tears. "Oh, you're making this so hard. I have a wonderful life in Virginia. My business is successful and my daughters are happy," I replied. Now tears were blurring my eyes. "If I stay longer my leaving will be much more difficult. You are unique and I never realized lovemaking could be so tender, so profound. The unexpected has happened and I'm falling in love with you. However, I'm not sure you are ready for a serious relationship. It is too soon after your divorce and separation from your young son. We both need time to think about where we go from here."

We were both miserable saying good-bye at the airport and acknowledged the difficulty of continuing a relationship with thousands of miles separating us. We embraced a final time without promises or guarantees, savoring the precious days we had together.

Bud called me the following morning as I was leaving for work. He said he couldn't sleep after saying good-bye. "I am the first to admit my life has been in turmoil over my separation from my young son, Shane. I dream about you even though my Censor, whom I try hard to ignore, comes across loud and clear." Bud added, "My Censor says, *'Orr, so much for keeping your life simple. Your divorce is not final and here you go looking for a reason to see Fran again. I hope you realize she is not another one night tumble in the sheets. I hope to God you know what the hell you are doing! You are not ready for love or any type of commitment.'"*

Needless to say I thought his Censor understood our situation perfectly. Before hanging up the telephone Bud told me he was spending more time with his squadron, the VA-97 Warhawks. He added that he had even completed overdue paperwork, volunteered for more flight time and occasionally stood extra duty, preferring the squadron environment to the emptiness of his apartment. He told me, "I can still smell the sweet, fresh scent of your body lingering on my sheets."

A week after I had returned the telephone was ringing when I opened the front door of my home in Virginia Beach. Bud called to invite me for another weekend visit. He said, "I was thrilled to hear the *USS Enterprise* and the airwing would be going to San Diego after an at-sea training exercise. While we are in San Diego the airwing will hold several informal parties that will culminate in a formal ball on Coronado Island. You are going to love Coronado. It is a small picturesque island community between San Diego Bay and the Pacific Ocean. Please come and please bring a formal and a couple of party dresses."

I could tell Bud was relieved when he heard laughter in my voice and realized he had convinced me to book a flight to San Diego for the following weekend.

Bud called back the next morning. "Fran, I want you to come to San Diego, but as I rolled out of bed this morning and headed for the shower I couldn't evade the nagging thoughts whirling around inside my head. I want to be with you but let's go slow and try to keep our relationship casual for the time being."

Without actually saying it I knew he was trying to tell me he was very certain that the part of his anatomy which seemed to be helping him make his decisions wanted to see me again. My heart had already committed to our relationship and, even though Bud wanted to believe it was casual, his actions spoke louder than his words, especially when he whispered how he longed for the warmth of my body and the tender, sweet taste of my lips.

The only issue before booking my flight was to tell my business partner I was returning to California. Deborah exclaimed, "Are you crazy? We are getting ready to open a second boutique. Look at how successful we are. Don't you care?"

She continued to ask good questions, but I didn't have the answers she wanted to hear. My heart was committed and led me to believe I was doing the right thing. Fortunately my brain did not interfere.

After my flight landed in San Diego, I was able to contact Bud in the Warhawks' ready room aboard the aircraft carrier. I let him know I was taking a taxi to the Navy Lodge on Coronado Island where he had reservations. He asked a squadron mate, Jeff (Bones) Ashby, to give me the keys to his room when I arrived. Bones was a junior officer who worked for Bud in the maintenance department of the VA-97 Warhawks. Later in his Navy career Bones would become an astronaut shuttle pilot. He met me at the Navy Lodge and gave me the key to the room so I could unpack and change clothes for the evening.

Bones told me Bud had asked him to escort me to Mexican Village on Coronado Island. He explained Bud was held up on the ship with some maintenance gripes and would be a little late. He smiled, "Bud told me that some women can get all whiney about going places unescorted but not his Fran."

Before I could respond he quickly explained, "Oops, you're not his Fran—yet.

"He says the two of you plan to go slow and keep your relationship casual. However, from the squadron's perspective, his actions seem to say something entirely different."

He added, "The squadron enjoys having dinner at Mexican Village whenever we are in town. It has been a favorite hangout for naval aviators since before the Vietnam War. The place is casual with a warm friendly atmosphere and if you like Mexican food you are in for a real treat. Let's wait in the bar until Bud arrives and while we wait you will have an opportunity to say hello to the squadron as they arrive."

I immediately felt Bud's presence as he walked into Mexican Village. He spotted me and his eyes embraced me. From the expression on his face he apparently liked what he saw. I was sitting at the bar with Bones and Captain Carol C. Smith, the Commanding Officer of the *USS Enterprise*. I was wearing a pale lavender leather halter top that was soft and feminine. I could feel Bud's touch as he ran his hand lightly across my back. He pulled me close indicating he liked the smooth, delicate feel of my body.

When the Warhawks sat down for dinner, Captain Smith joined the squadron at Bud's invitation. I don't remember what we ate but would always remember Bud's warmth as he let his hand slide along my thigh. When the band started playing, he was eager to get me onto the dance floor and into his arms. Whether we danced slow or fast we moved together as one, our bodies instinctually responding to the music.

He whispered, "The moment I walked in the door and saw you the jolt to my loins was instantaneous. I was positive it would happen. I'm one lucky sonofabitch!" I looked up at him and gave him a long slow smile, uncertain how to tell him he was having the same impact on me.

He continued to hold me close and in a husky voice said, "God, I just want to take you out of here." He didn't say it, but I was sure he meant into bed. We were both absolutely certain bedtime was not going to happen any time soon.

The guys broke in to dance with me several times just to tease Bud. Doing so also gave them an opportunity to become better acquainted with me. Captain Smith also asked me to dance. While the Captain and I danced Bud watched him talking intently. Later in the evening, he asked me about our conversation. I answered, "He told me you are a remarkable young man with multiple talents. One of your special gifts is the ability to see the man within the uniform. He said whether he observed you talking to an officer or an enlisted man, you always treat them with equal interest and respect."

When Bud completed his first command tour the squadron gift was a scrapbook. In the introduction of the scrapbook the squadron wrote, *"My pilots call me Skipper, my wife calls me Bud, my men call me anytime."*

While I was on the dance floor Bud dutifully danced with a couple of the squadron wives who were sitting patiently beside husbands who didn't dance or were busy telling flying stories with their hands in the air.

Bud had a reputation for being one of the last to leave a party, but not this night. As the first couple from the squadron stood up to say good-night, Bud and I joined them as they exited the restaurant. Bud said the guys would tease him about his early departure, but tonight he didn't care.

Love at First Flight

We took a cab back to the Navy Lodge. Bud pulled me into his arms as soon as he gave the driver instructions where to take us. I was as eager and needy for him as he was for me. As we arrived at the Lodge Bud shoved some cash into the cab driver's hand and headed for our room, which had a water view but the view from inside was all either one of us was interested in seeing. The view we had been dreaming about for weeks was of me slowly undressing and lying naked in bed. We touched, caressed, kissed and explored each other as our clothing fell to the floor. Bud wanted me and thankfully my passionate response gave way to the sensual dance of love. We were hurled into the heavens, gradually descending where all is calm and light, drifting into a beautiful, peaceful slumber.

11
Gopher Holes—Not So Easy

I AWAKENED EARLY THE FOLLOWING MORNING with Bud asleep, holding me in his arms. I woke him with a gentle caress and said, "It is a beautiful cool day and we have time to enjoy a quiet walk on the beach." As we walked together hand in hand I watched Bud take every opportunity to engage in friendly conversation with someone walking past who appeared interesting. Pet owners always received extra attention. I laughed, enjoying the unpredictability of being with him. "I believe it is impossible for you to walk past a dog without wanting to pat the canine's head or let it lick your face or hand."

"I have always had a desire to meet new people and a fondness for most dogs. For some reason I feel the need to let the owner know I think they have chosen a wonderful pet."

In the evening we joined the Airwing at the Chart House across the street from the famous Hotel del Coronado for an evening of camaraderie, drinking and dancing. It was late when we left the Chart House and arrived at the Navy Lodge. I said, "I remember seeing a silly picture of you and two friends sitting on your fireplace mantle. I'm interested in hearing the story behind the picture."

Love at First Flight

Bud said he remembered the picture I asked about. The three men in the picture were wearing sunglasses, had girlie scarves wrapped around their heads, and were making a toast holding a mug of beer in their hands. "The picture is of me with my friends Jesse James and Mike Bowman. Later in his Navy career Mike became a three-star Admiral and remains one of my closest personal friends. Jesse flew into the ground and killed himself." Bud added, "I don't want to talk about Jesse right now. I think you will enjoy the story of how I got the temporary call sign *Gopher.*" Bud made sure I was comfortable and began his story by reminding me that on his first combat cruise he served with VA-113 Stingers aboard the *USS Enterprise*.

I turned to Fran and said, "In the early part of the cruise the squadron was scheduled to fly sorties in support of the U.S. Marine Corps' small staging base in Khe Sanh, South Vietnam. Khe Sanh was one of the most remote outposts in Vietnam and in 1968 the military brass were trying to decide whether to hold the staging base, or quietly abandoned it. The Marines were under a full-scale siege from the Viet Cong and the question went all the way to President Lyndon Johnson. The answer came back, hold the base."

The Carrier Airwing Commander, CAG Paul Peck, was leading a flight of four aircraft on a *close air support mission* and I was his wingman on the air strike. As the flight approached Khe Sanh, the Forward Air Controller (FAC) warned the pilots we would be operating in very close proximity to friendlies. The FAC wanted to ensure the safety of the Marines by advising CAG Peck to have the pilots hone their bombing accuracy. The Viet Cong had dug tunnels all around the airfield in Khe Sanh, launched an effective attack and were very close to overwhelming the small Marine base.

The Stingers were flying brand new Douglas A-4F Skyhawks with the newest CP-741 automatic bomb release system. The bomb release system allowed a pilot to put the gun sight on a target on zero mils instead of a preset computed setting for a prescribed dive angle, airspeed and release altitude. At the appropriate altitude the pilot presses the bomb pickle on the stick and applies four to five g's on the aircraft and pulls up. The computer would release the bombs at the appropriate point to optimize the bomb hitting the target.

Gopher Holes—Not So Easy

To counter the full-sized siege and tunneling threat by the Viet Cong each Skyhawk was loaded with three one-thousand-pound Mark-83 bombs. The bombs had stainless steel noses with electric tail fuses. The bombs penetrated the ground with the sharp stainless steel nose and burrow twenty-six feet underground. Deep underground, the electric fuse would energize the explosion of the one thousand pounds of explosives, wreaking havoc with the Viet Cong tunnels.

I was always cautious operating near friendlies and wanted to make sure I did not fuck up and kill our own Marines. As our flight approached the target we saw a C-130 Hercules cargo transport aircraft take off from the Marine airfield. The Hercules was hit by small arms fire, blew apart and crashed. The mission was off to a fiery beginning.

I rolled in behind CAG Peck and put my Skyhawk into a forty-five-degree dive and placed the center of the gun site on the target which had been marked by FAC with *Willy-Pete* white phosphorous smoke rocket. I held the aircraft in the dive interminably past the safe pull out to adjust my aim point and also to ensure the safety of the friendlies in the area.

Finally I was satisfied and pressed the red bomb button on the stick and eased on a five-g pull. I had two two-thousand-pound drop tanks with remaining fuel in them, a full bag of internal fuel and three one-thousand-pound bombs. The small A-4 was extremely heavy and continued to mush toward the ground. I was past the release point and none of the bombs had come off. I could see the ground coming up in my peripheral vision. At full power, nose up and still descending I saw dirt and rocks flying around my aircraft. All I could do was hold my angle of attack and pray my aircraft would start to climb before hitting the ground. I heard the cling-cling of rocks and dirt hitting the Skyhawk's turbine blades as the aircraft flew through the debris of CAG's bombs going off twenty-six feet underground. I held my breath as the heavy A-4 began to climb and the Skyhawk's rate of descent was neutralized. I watched in relief as the vertical speed indicator gauge registered my aircraft was indeed climbing.

I returned to the pattern to give the bombing run another try. Not smart—in fact, it was a DUMB idea. I approached the target with a more conservative pattern by not pressing the target and again, no bombs left my aircraft. CAG Peck came up on the radio and said, "Battlecry 302, divert to Da Nang."

I pointed my aircraft toward the Tonkin Gulf and made a simulated bombing run over the water in a final attempt to jettison the three one-thousand-pound bombs and the bomb rack all at once. Again, nothing dropped off my aircraft. By now I realized my aircraft had a blown master armament fuse which precluded even jettisoning the bomb racks from my aircraft. It would be unsafe to land aboard the ship with two drop tanks and three one-thousand-pound armed bombs.

I navigated the Skyhawk down the South Vietnamese coastline until I identified the entry into Da Nang Harbor. I then contacted the Marine Air Traffic Controller at the Da Nang Marine Air Station and relayed the circumstances of my emergency and the urgency to land the Skyhawk. It would be necessary to make a very heavy landing with hung ordinance. Concurrently, I was approaching an ominous black cloud belching with lightning and rain. The cloud hung between my aircraft and the Da Nang Marine Air Station.

The Air Traffic Controller picked me up on radar and vectored me toward the duty runway, which just happened to take me directly into the thunderstorm. I had no other alternative but to continue my approach towards the airfield. By now I was low on fuel and would be forced to land soon. Landing in the torrential rain dictated an arrested landing similar to landing aboard the aircraft carrier. I touched down at one hundred and fifty knots, and the Skyhawk hydroplaned into the arresting gear wire and shuddered nose down to a violent stop.

I sat strapped inside the cockpit for several minutes, contemplating the myriad of challenges I had encountered throughout the day. I was relieved to be on the ground, and when I opened the cockpit I let the rain fall on my face and took a moment to unwind. I was cleared by Air Traffic Control to taxi into the Marine Corps flight line. The sky cleared, the sun came out and I felt like a new person. Not so fast, Big Boy!

The Marine Corps F-4 Phantom squadron had been designated to take care of me so I turned my aircraft and started to taxi slowly toward their flight line. Two young Marine red shirts met my aircraft on the taxiway to insert safety pins in the bomb racks. The safety pins ensured my bombs would not accidentally jettison on the runway. Once the ordnance men completed their task, I was directed by ground control to taxi to the front of the Marine Corps hangar.

Gopher Holes—Not So Easy

Off to my right I saw a high-power turn up test stand with an F-4 Phantom bellowing black smoke out of its big J-79 Pratt and Whitney engines into the jet blast deflector. The JBD on the airfield in Da Nang was a similar deflector to what was used on the aircraft carrier.

I happened to look up just as the Phantom went into afterburner in both engines. Fire was belching out of the tailpipes instead of just smoke. Then all HELL broke loose! The tie down chains broke under the strain of the powerful F-4 afterburner engines and the aircraft literally leaped out of the test stand onto the taxiway. The aircraft was clearly out of control. The pilot attempted to stop by pushing hard on the brakes. I stopped my Skyhawk in shock and awe at the incredible sight I was witnessing as the F-4 Phantom careened toward me.

The Phantom continued to screech toward my aircraft, leaving black tire marks. The tires blew and still the jet lunged forward on the rims of the wheels with sparks flying! It was happening so fast. All I could imagine was what a shitty way to die after all I had just been through. Already it looked as if I would be rammed by a runaway Phantom in afterburner, with me sitting in a small jet carrying three thousand pounds of live bombs and full of fuel.

Then the F-4 took a turn toward the hangar, lurching forward on the rims of the aircraft's wheels. Finally, just before hitting the hangar the F-4 seemed to decelerate, the engines shut down and it stopped just short of collision.

I was extremely shaken by the incident but continued to taxi my aircraft in front of the hangar where maintenance personnel were signaling me to park. Needless to say I was anxious to get out of my aircraft and find out what the fuck had happened to the Phantom. After the maintenance crewmen put chocks in front of the wheels of my A-4 they signaled for me to shut the engine down on my aircraft. I was elated and relieved to be out harm's way as I lifted myself out of the cockpit, climbed down the ladder and touched the ground.

The senior ordnance crewman told me it would take about an hour for the red shirts to offload my bombs before I would be ready to return to the *Enterprise*. I walked among the crowd of Marines encircling the Phantom pilot that had exited the silenced F-4. I made my way up to the front of the group and amazingly recognized the pilot. Marine First Lieutenant Dick (Easy) Easley had been a classmate of mine in flight training command at Saufley Field, Pensacola, Florida. I had not seen Easy since the training command and approached him with a warm greeting. After a brief exchange, I asked, "What the hell just happened?"

Easy explained that somehow while performing a high-power turn up, the F-4 Phantom inadvertently went into afterburner and leaped out of the chocks. As the engines continued to run, he shut off the fuel master switches. By closing off the fuel supply to the engines, the F-4 finally ran out of gas and shut down.

I knew the Phantom was one of the few Navy fighters that actually had fuel on/off switches inside the cockpit. What a lucky day for Easy, and I was certainly one lucky sonofabitch to have survived the day.

I manned my Skyhawk, refueled in the fuel pits and taxied out to the runway for the return flight back to the safety of the *"Big E"* without my bombs. I had experienced more than my share of excitement for one day.

After landing aboard the aircraft carrier I went down to the ready room. Lieutenant Don Williams, later in his Navy career a famous *Challenger* astronaut and shuttle pilot, greeted me. Don was number three in the *close air support mission* and was right behind CAG and me at Khe Sanh. Don said, "I watched you go very low and disappear into the dirt kicked up by CAG's bombs. It looked just like a giant gopher stuck his head up, shook it and you flew through the debris the burrowing land tortoise kicked up. Your new call sign is *Gopher*!"

As Bud finished the story I was laughing at the image he had depicted to earn a new call sign. At one point during the story I felt compelled to stop him and say, "I'm so glad you didn't die. You were so young to have so many traumatic experiences and live with the possibility of death, every time you catapulted off of the aircraft carrier. When you were flying in harm's way, I was a young single mother barely aware of the men dying in a faraway place called Vietnam. A war was being fought and I didn't even know the reason we were there. I recalled a time when my church harbored an AWOL soldier who wanted to become a conscientious objector. It attracted enough local attention to be mentioned on the evening news."

Although I was disappointed, Bud still felt the need to let me know he wanted to keep our relationship casual. His actions, however, conveyed something completely different. I was willing to risk my heart to spend more time with a man I found fascinating, irresistible and made no pretense that I didn't see the warmth and desire sparkling in his eyes.

12

Jesse James

THE NEXT MORNING BUD WENT FOR a run while I stayed in bed. Before leaving he said, "I'm tempted to forgo my run and continue to lie by your side but I think you need the rest after me keeping you awake talking about myself."

I was standing in the small kitchenette of our room when he returned from his run. I was wearing his squadron tee shirt and little else. Bud greeted me with his easy smile, "I've decided my tee shirt looks a hell of a lot better on you than on me."

Every glance from him made me feel desirable and beautiful. I poured a glass of orange juice and sat a plate of fresh fruit and a bagel in front of him before serving myself. I was delighted with how comfortable we were with each other.

We finished eating and Bud said, "I want to know more about you and your life in Virginia Beach."

"Okay, I'll share more if you promise to tell me the story about your best friend, Jesse James."

"You don't give up, do you? I'll try but I don't like to think about what happened to Jesse. Let me take a quick shower and I'll join you shortly."

When he returned I was sitting on the sofa. My eyes closed, savoring how peaceful and serene I felt. I was aware of Bud's presence as he entered the room. I slowly opened my eyes as he stood quietly staring at me, enjoying the moment. He whispered in a voice laden with feelings, "Are you always this peaceful? You look so beautiful silhouetted against the morning light coming through the window. As I entered the room I felt as if I walked into pure sunshine and I want to savor this magic moment." He stood reverently before adding, "I'm so grateful for a blind date that has become precious to me. I can already feel how difficult it will be to let you go."

He knelt in front of me, easing me slowly down onto the rug. We became lost in our feelings as he took me into a gentle embrace, guiding me into the passion and fire that was gloriously burning. We climbed willingly into the flame, found release and fell asleep in one another's arms.

Bud opened his eyes, feeling a chill in the room as he realized I had taken away the comfort and warmth of my body lying next to him. I stood in the doorway, looking down into his clear blue eyes smiling up at me. It was my time to admire his solid, athletic body and said in a teasing voice, "You can leave your pants off if you want, but you did promise me another story."

Bud laughed, stood up irreverently and pulled on his jeans, "As soon as I hear a little more about your life, your wish will be my command."

"I was praying that we could forget about me and move on to another story. Your life is much more interesting and every day is an adventure for you. Let me share another reason I came to California and how we happened to go on a blind date."

Without going into many details I told him about my search for a Jungian analyst for psychotherapy. My minister put me in contact with a psychiatrist in New York who recommended an analyst in my area. There were days I left his office elated and so proud of my progress but there were other times when I knew I hadn't done my part. Along with my therapy sessions I attended Virginia Wesleyan College part time. Some sessions I just wanted to talk about school and after I left his office I realized I had avoided my reason for seeing him. I needed to come to terms with my abusive childhood and abandonment issues.

Dr. Kledzik worked with me for five years in both private and group sessions. He believed in me and taught me to trust in myself until I regained the strength and confidence to journey into my past. He calmly and patiently allowed me to wait until I was ready to let my inner demons show themselves. The demons of heartache, cruelty, loneliness and others I had buried in my subconscious. He also taught me to remember that I am the master of my thoughts.

Dr. Kledzik promised that by cultivating and weeding out harmful thoughts I would become the caretaker of a precious garden, a garden that was always present within, no matter how I was choked with despair, failure and pain. He provided me with the seeds of promise, to attain the life I wanted if I focused on positive thoughts to realize my dreams. I used visualization to see my future as if it already existed. Through practice I learned to plant healthy thoughts and was rewarded with happiness as I watched the flowers of positive energy push through the fertile ground.

During one of my final sessions Dr. Kledzik suggested I take a vacation. Between taking care of my daughters, my career, church and school I was left with very little free time. He suggested I go alone, so when Jim invited me to California it seemed a perfect opportunity to spread my wings.

"Enough about me; I really want to hear about your friend, Jesse."

Jesse and I returned from our first Western Pacific combat cruise full of confidence. We radiated that indestructible *"they can't kill me"* attitude. We had returned from combat having flown the new Douglas A4-F Skyhawk. The squadron traded the Skyhawks in and began slowly taking delivery of the new A7-B Corsair II aircraft. The older Skyhawks would be used by the Navy Reserve or sold to one of our country's allies. A complete acceptance flight test was required each time a new A7-B from Ling Temco Vought in Dallas, Texas, was delivered to the Lemoore Naval Air Station. The test flight on the new aircraft was performed by a designated squadron test pilot. *Indestructible* Jesse had qualified as one of the squadron test pilots shortly after returning from our Western Pacific combat cruise.

He took off by himself from the Lemoore Naval Air Station on a late afternoon in a new A7-B Corsair II to perform the required test flight. Jesse flew northeast from Lemoore toward Fallon, Nevada, and over sparsely populated Owens Valley to perform the test on the new aircraft. One of the superfluous tests was a supersonic run. The test was a chore for the chubby, under-powered Corsair. Jesse climbed to twenty thousand feet, pointed the nose of the aircraft straight down and held the throttle at full power until achieving the magic Mach I airspeed of approximately seven hundred miles per hour before he pulled out.

After completing the test, Jesse saw a truck driving down the Owens Valley Highway near Mono Lake. In his exuberance he decided to make a simulated strafing run. The accident investigation statement from the truck driver read, "As the pilot made his second low pass I was scared so badly I defecated in my pants." After that pass Jesse pulled up sharply and the tail of his aircraft impacted a small rise in the high desert floor. The accident investigation determined that when the tail pipe impacted the ground the aircraft exploded. The explosion caused an inadvertent ejection of Jesse from the cockpit.

After the death of Whiskey-Man in the early months of my first combat cruise, I had learned how to deal with tragedy. However, I was not prepared to mourn the loss of my best friend. I volunteered to escort Jesse's body home to his family in Ohio to give myself an opportunity to accept and grieve another loss.

Transportation of Jesse's body was held up in San Francisco at the Oakland Naval Hospital. I was told to wait before transporting his body home for burial. At the request of the family, their Congressman had called the Office of Legislative Affairs (OLA) in Washington, D.C., to ascertain the cause of the delay. I cannot recall what the naval officer in OLA gave as the reason for the delay to the grieving family. The reason for the hold-up was because the naval accident investigators had located Jesse's arm near the crash site. The Navy would not allow the body to be transported until all remains recovered were sent home for burial at one time.

It was twenty years later when I served in the United States Senate as Principle Deputy of the Senate Liaison Office of Legislative Affairs that I understood the role of the Congressman and the naval officer at OLA. A great deal of effort, time, equipment and people went into ensuring our fallen military have an honorable and proper burial.

I was in tears as I remembered the loss of such an exciting, dynamic and talented pilot and friend. I said to Fran, "Sometimes the pain from the past hurts so bad that the loss consumes everything as we realize how deeply we cared. One morning we awaken and acknowledge they are gone forever and life must move on."

I found myself in the role of comforter. In a soothing voice and holding Bud tenderly in my arms I reminded him, "Remember the picture you showed me of Mike, Jesse and you laughing and clowning together?"

Bud only nodded his head.

"Well, the photograph captured a special time, a silly moment between friends, yet a moment to be savored forever." I smiled and softly brushed his lips. "The pain of the past will always be a part of who you are, but your response to the pain is what matters most. I think it is important to celebrate such a friendship and you have been lucky to experience more than one in your lifetime."

I added, "I remember a comment I read somewhere written by a World War II pilot upon the death of a friend. The thought was, *'Jesse's wings are forever folded. When he awakened in heaven his arrival caused the stars to shine a little brighter.'*"

Before my return trip home to Virginia, Bud made reservations at the famous and historic Hotel del Coronado for us to enjoy an elegant Sunday brunch. He wore his Navy whites with ribbons. I watched several heads turn as we entered the hotel. I said, "I feel honored to have a handsome naval aviator walking beside me."

Bud told me the famous movie *Some Like It Hot*, starring Jack Lemmon and Marilyn Monroe, was filmed in the lobby of the hotel in the 1960s. I replied, "I think the impact of a military man in uniform and what it represents to people in the lobby is more significant than a funny Hollywood movie could have been." We followed the maître d' to a table with a water view. Bud smiled at the guests who thanked him for his service to our country.

In the afternoon I asked Bud to call a taxi for my return trip to the airport. I did not want to repeat another tearful and miserable good-bye. I called him after arriving in Virginia and told him, "As I crossed over the Coronado Bay Bridge into San Diego on my journey home I allowed the tears to fall. I feel as if a part of my heart has been left on the enchanting island on the bay."

"I understand," he said. "Once I was back aboard the *Enterprise* I was trying to figure out what to do about a blind date I can't forget."

13

A Rough Start

When I met Fran I was so taken back by her beauty and grace I felt humbled to be in her presence. That seems to never change. As the reality of the challenges of her childhood became clear I searched my soul in an attempt to discover what I had done to deserve my life. I have been given so much and with so little effort. I still marvel at how disciplined and smart Fran is to have evolved from an unimaginable childhood, to such a gracious young woman through her private search for what was right and proper. Of course her spirituality gave her strength, but it was her ability to learn quickly from others and collate the finer things of life into her persona that made her so well presented. She has always been a voracious reader and has been able to absorb material like a sponge, and transform it into her ever-evolving, radiant energy.

For me, in retrospect and in comparison, my childhood was a walk along the riverbank. We had little, but wanted little. My youth was centered on the outdoors, rivers, creeks, lakes and the wilderness of the beautiful state of Oregon. All were within walking distance of my home and were my playground. School always had the same people moving through the grades until the third grade when Tom Hathaway showed up. He said his family had just moved from another town. I thought, "Whoever heard of moving from one town to another?" I thought it very strange! I had never known anyone who had moved.

Our little town of six thousand people stayed pretty much the same year after year and the idea of moving to another house, let alone another town, was total anathema. In fact, I lived in the same house my whole life, with my two sisters, one older and one younger, until going off to college. I never saw a black man until we visited our cousins in Los Angeles when I was nine.

Later I found out that when community concerts came to Grants Pass the black members of the orchestra were required to stay outside the city limits. This was done quietly and not discussed. No doubt we were as much or more prejudiced than any city in the Deep South. Again, this subject was never talked about in my home. The good news is that I was never *brainwashed* with prejudice, as was often the case when from one generation to the next took on the hatred of their parents. I left home for college untainted.

My naivety was one reason that I was able to move into a multicultural and highly prejudicial military in the sixties, and still be able to maintain and resist prejudice throughout my life. I had never even met a Jewish person until my father took me to college and dropped me at my dormitory. He noted that my roommate's name was Ralph Cohen. He lowered his head and quietly hissed, "He's a Jew." The comment clearly showed my father's prejudice, but it had not been transmitted to me.

So, my seemingly boring childhood was actually fulfilling, but not without trauma. At age eleven, I was in the front yard of my neighbor Butch Parker's house. From about twenty feet away he was shooting a BB gun at my feet, and I was shooting a homemade bow and arrow, made from willows and kite string, at his feet. As I released the crooked arrow it took flight upward rather than down and to my horror struck him in the eye. The arrow dropped to the ground and blood was gushing between his fingers as he rushed for the front door. I begged him not to go in, saying, "It will be okay."

I ran home and barged onto our back porch where my mother stood ironing our clothes on the red concrete floor. I yelled, "Mom, I hit Butch Parker in the eye with an arrow."

She dropped the iron and screamed, "Oh my Lord!"

We ran out of the house to our car. She knew Butch's mother did not drive and had no way to transport Butch to the hospital. Mom drove around the block and picked up Butch and his mother and raced to the hospital. In the following weeks Butch was restricted to his parents' living room, which was kept dark. They had draped an old Army blanket across the front window to keep the light out in an effort to save his eye. But the effort was to no avail. The doctors put in a glass eye. I read in a newspaper column in the *Daily Courier* that my father was sued for five thousand dollars, an enormous sum of money at the time. I cried silently, feeling ashamed, lost and alone in my room.

Butch was a grade ahead of me in our only high school. I played sports; Butch was the water boy. For the rest of my life as I ran through brush or anything came in contact with one of my eyes I would hold my hand close to my face as tears fell warmly against my fingers. I was afraid to open my eyes for fear that I would see blood rather than tears. I worried for years about the bible quotation *"An eye for an eye."*

College was a different story. I pledged the top fraternity and found myself to be popular for whatever reason. Streams, rivers and mountains were replaced by classrooms, fraternity parties and pretty girls. On summer break I came home and often stayed out late after being over served. I was very intoxicated as I opened the back door and ran headlong into my father.

"Where the hell have you been?" he asked.

I gave him the truth, "Out with a carhop from Larry's Drive Inn."

It was sometime later my mother confided that my father's greatest worry was that I would get some girl pregnant and ruin my life. She said that looking back on that evening she thought he might have had a mild heart attack. If so, it was one of several he would have later in life.

After a minor setback in my junior year and flunking out of school because of having too much fun, I returned to graduate with a degree in Public Relations, Journalism and Advertising. From college to commissioning in Newport Rhode Island and flight school in Pensacola Florida I was on my way to fulfilling my grandest dream.

Who were these guys from the Naval Academy? They seemed like children. They raged around in their new cars, with two of them killing themselves by driving off the Pensacola Bridge drunk. They seemed so unpolished. They were very smart in class, but extremely unfinished and wild outside of class. They wore white socks with dark suits and seemed to be void of any social protocols. And they were! In the sixties the academies were tightly controlled for at least the first three years. The middies had very little access to social activities outside of preplanned events. It was almost as if they had been in jail for four years and now that they were out they were trying to make up for what they had missed. As the years passed, they became socially adept and, of course, their talent and heritage provided a wonderful platform for promotion to the Navy's highest ranks, for those who survived.

14

Weird Harold

Fran did not like to spend time on the telephone, so conversations each night were never long enough for me. To keep from missing her so much I wrote and told her of my adventures.

I began, "It was 11:30 at night on the end of runway three two left at Naval Air Station Lemoore. The airfield had a right and left runway and three two zero was the magnetic heading of the runway in use. Naval Air Station Lemoore was in the San Joaquin Valley, in Central California. It was a flat, lushly irrigated, inland valley which came alive at harvest time. During the Vietnam War Naval Air Station Lemoore had more aviators who were prisoners of war, missing-in-action or killed than any other base in the United States." Today, NAS Lemoore remains the largest Naval Air Station in the country, flying the premier Boeing FA-18 Super Hornets.

I was sitting at a small metal table with Lieutenant Junior Grade Kurt (Hitman) Hetterman, who was training to become a landing signal officer (LSO). We were watching six single-seat A7-B Corsair IIs come into the break for landing. The pilots on approach were practicing night field carrier landings, preparing for day and night carrier qualifications in the brand new Ling Temco Vought A7-B Corsairs II.

My Navy squadron, the VA-113 Stingers, had recently returned from the Western Pacific and combat operations aboard the *USS Enterprise*. The squadron traded in their Douglas A4-F Skyhawks and had gone through transition training in the A7-B Corsair IIs with the VA-122 Flying Eagles. VA-122 was the Replacement Air Group (RAG) training squadron in Lemoore. The Stingers would detach from Carrier Air Group Nine aboard the *USS Enterprise,* home ported in Alameda, California. The squadron was reassigned to Carrier Air Group Three on the *USS Saratoga,* home ported in Mayport, Florida, and join the VA-46 Clansman to take the first A7-Bs into the Mediterranean.

During the Vietnam War, in the early 1970s, the Navy decided to transition more East coast squadrons into combat operations. The West coast squadrons had sustained tremendous losses of pilots and aircraft throughout the mid- to late 1960s. The Navy made the decision to reassign several West Coast squadrons to the Mediterranean while the East coast squadrons would make the transition into the Western Pacific and have their opportunity to fly in combat, be shot at and earn some air medals. Being reassigned to the East coast sounded like a good idea to me. The Mediterranean with its crystal clear water, white sandy beaches and the opportunity to meet gorgeous bikini-clad women was much more appealing than my experiences of flying in the Tonkin Gulf with the ever-present danger of being shot down, captured or killed.

Back on the end of runway three two left the evening was a typical autumn night in the San Joaquin Valley: cool, light winds, slight overcast on an inky dark night. All of the runway lights were turned off except those that reflected the outline of the angle deck on an aircraft carrier, a rectangular box of white lights with a centerline down the middle. Behind me, about thirty feet down the runway, was the Fresnel lens, a landing aid system composed of five square cells stacked on top of each other. The refraction was so clear and finite that a pilot in the groove (on final approach) could only see one light or cell at a time. A pilot could tell by the single yellow light, referred to as the *meatball,* relative to the stationary green datum lights flanking the center cell if he was high, low or centered perfectly on the glide path.

This was my life! I flew in the daytime and sat on the end of the runway at night, training the squadron pilots to fly the new A7-B Corsair II aboard the aircraft carrier, day and night. I watched and graded each pilot as they flew ten landings night after night, while still being haunted by the myriad of changes in my life. As the senior landing signal officer (LSO), my responsibility was to coach each pilot over the radio handset as his aircraft touched down and then grade each pass the same as it would be done aboard the aircraft carrier. I needed to stay totally focused as each pilot landed his aircraft and would debrief each landing grade with the pilots after flight operations were completed.

In addition to a pilot's field carrier landing practice during the daytime, each pilot was required to make ten practice landings every night for two weeks. Ten practice landings usually took about thirty minutes, with an LSO spending between two to three hours every night on the end of the runway. After a pilot completed ten night practice field carrier landings he would taxi his aircraft into the fuel pits and hot switch.

Fran called me when she got my letter and asked me, "What is a *hot switch*?"

I said, "You ask good questions. I'm so used to the navy jargon I sometimes forget to explain things clearly. *Hot switch* just means a pilot who gets into a jet with the engine running to relieve a pilot who has landed aboard the aircraft carrier."

The pilot who landed would refuel the aircraft to the appropriate landing weight, and with the jet engine still running a *hot switch* pilot would climb into the cockpit as the pilot who had completed his practice field carrier landings exited the aircraft. The *hot switch* pilot would perform a brief checklist of the aircraft's gauges and taxi out to the runway, take off and enter the practice field carrier landing pattern.

The pattern was flown at six hundred feet above ground level, just as pilots would do on the aircraft carrier, only on a carrier the aircraft was flown at six hundred feet above water. Each pilot in the landing pattern would approach a position abeam the LSO platform where Greg (Hitman) Hetterman and I were sitting. He would decelerate the aircraft from one hundred and fifty knots or one hundred and seventy-four miles per hour down to landing speed. The landing speed was programmed by the angle of attack indicator which determined the optimum landing speed for the gross weight of the aircraft. The gross weight was always, at or below the acceptable maximum gross weight for landing either on land or aboard the aircraft carrier.

A pilot would approach the simulated carrier flight deck just exactly as he would on an aircraft carrier underway. Everything would be the same as the carrier at sea except for the wind over the flight deck. The amount of wind over the deck was determined by the speed of the aircraft carrier moving through the water rather than the wind over the runway. Tonight, on runway three two left there was only the wind down the runway which was the best simulation of an aircraft carrier flight deck available on land.

I could see the arrival of an A7-B Corsair II smoking into the break at eight hundred feet, traveling three hundred and fifty miles per hour. The aircraft crossed the simulated aircraft carrier deck heading three hundred and twenty degrees. The pilot checked over his left shoulder to determine if he was at the proper interval behind the aircraft ahead of him. He looked to see if he was cleared to break at a point to begin his practice field carrier landing approximately one minute behind the aircraft in front of him. At the point where the aircraft the pilot was following was at his eight o'clock position he would crisply roll his Corsair into an eighty- to ninety-degree angle of bank. The pilot would pull back on the stick, while simultaneously reducing the power to near idle and ease about four g's on the aircraft.

"I remember you demonstrating g's by lying on top of me. If he pulled about four g's would that push him down into his seat?" Fran asked.

"That's right, and the process caused the Corsair to decelerate and allowed the pilot to turn his aircraft in the opposite direction of the runway to a heading of one hundred and forty degrees."

Next, the pilot decelerated below one hundred and eighty knots or two hundred eight miles per hour and held level at eight hundred feet above the ground. He lowered the landing gear and flaps and trimmed the aircraft as the Corsair continued to decelerate from one hundred and eighty knots to one hundred and fifty knots or one hundred and seventy-four miles per hour. He then descended from break altitude of eight hundred feet to six hundred feet above the ground. This was a big transition as the pilot constantly trimmed the Corsair to adjust to the reducing airspeed and increased stick pressure. Simultaneously he increased the angle of attack, and nose attitude.

When the Corsair approached the one-hundred-and-eighty-degree position abeam of the LSO platform I watched closely as the pilot continued to decelerate his aircraft to approach speed. On his first approach in the pattern he would check in with the LSO. Paddles is the Navy nickname for all landing signal officers.

"Paddles, 305 at the one eighty with six thousand pounds of fuel, Weird." Lieutenant Junior Grade (Weird) Harold Smith was the pilot on approach.

Each pilot would check in with the LSO using his call sign and the number of his aircraft. It was very important for the LSO to identify each pilot in the pattern in order for him to grade each landing and ensure the pilot would be debriefed correctly.

The practice field carrier night landings were going smoothly. Aircraft were entering and departing the pattern at appropriate intervals. The wind was constant at about ten to twelve miles per hour right down the runway. Hitman and I were enjoying the cool breeze and the pleasant night. Nevertheless, CAUTION—never forget flying is dangerous business! Single-seat fighter pilots flying at six hundred feet above the ground at night (with no visible horizon) know they must never relax!

Weird was on his third approach in aircraft 305 and was passing the one-hundred-and-eighty-degree position or abeam the LSO platform at six hundred feet. He waited twelve seconds before he started turning his Corsair toward the runway. Weird began his descent to arrive at the ninety-degree position at four hundred and fifty feet and looked out the portside of his cockpit and saw the yellow *meatball* landing aid system on the Fresnel lens.

As Weird continued his turn the Corsair intercepted the centerline in a gentle, gradual descent of four to six hundred feet per minute. He arrived in the groove at one-quarter mile. Paddles heard the call, "305 Corsair ball, state three thousand, five hundred pounds, Weird."

My return call was "Roger ball, you're looking good."

One of the many challenges pilots needed to practice at the field was close-in wave-offs. The flight deck on an aircraft carrier at sea is always a busy place and you never knew when intentionally or inadvertently a person, aircraft or piece of equipment would end up in the landing area and foul the flight deck, making the aircraft unsafe to land. Pilots must always be prepared for a foul deck wave-off, even though the intensity of a close-in approach would almost max him out. The cockpit work load for Weird flying the Corsair was at its peak.

Weird was due for a practice wave-off. I waited until the aircraft's wheels were about a hundred feet off the runway. I pushed the LSO pickle button to activate the wave-off lights which caused bright flashing red lights to illuminate both sides and the top of the Fresnel lens. Simultaneously I called on the radio handset, "Foul deck! Wave-off!"

Weird did well. He rapidly advanced the power of the Corsair to one hundred percent and set the angle of attack to ensure a safe fly away. He passed the LSO platform at full power, engine screaming as the A7-B climbed rapidly. The wheels cleared the runway by only feet.

As Weird continued his climb to six hundred feet Hitman and I turned to observe the completion of the wave-off and observed a bright flash of sparks pouring out of the tailpipe of his Corsair II followed immediately by total silence. As we watched intently the lights on the A7-B went out. I ran to the edge of the runway trying in vain to see Weird's aircraft in the darkness.

Hitman and I heard the blast and saw the rocket of the ejection seat propelling Weird up at twenty g's, and then everything around the airfield was dark and quiet. Within what seemed like seconds there was a tremendous explosion and a yellow mushroom of light, smoke and a huge fireball down the runway. We could see Weird silhouetted by the fire, hanging in his parachute about two hundred feet above the runway. The fire was burning ferociously in what looked to be directly below him. It appeared he was going to land in the flames.

I immediately threw down my handset and pickle and started running full speed down the center of the dark runway toward the inferno. My heart was pounding rapidly. I thought, "I can't believe what I am seeing—Weird has landed in the flames of his own aircraft." Then, BLAM, I found myself stumbling and rolling down the runway. I had run headlong into Weird strapped into his torso harness, still attached to his parachute. The parachute lines were dragging him further down the runway toward the flames.

Fortunately Weird was safe and was taken by ambulance to the base hospital for a complete physical check-up and evaluation by the flight surgeon. He sustained a few minor bruises and was able to return to the flight schedule several days later.

Flight operations were cancelled for the remainder of the night to clear the debris from the runway. After every aircraft accident there is an investigation to discover the cause of the accident. The report determined the A7-B Corsair sustained foreign object damage. The engine was deemed to have ingested foreign matter, such as a piece of a blown tire, into the large intake during one of the practice landings. The following morning flight training resumed.

15
Cross-Country Courtship

PRIOR TO THE FUEL SHORTAGE IN the early 1970s, in order for pilots to get extra flight time it was standard procedure for them to schedule cross country training. A cross country flight would give the pilot experience in navigation and refueling at various Navy and Air Force bases across the country. The cross country flights also gave a pilot carte blanche to take *his own Navy jet* to visit relatives or friends anywhere in the continental United States.

Virginia was beginning to seem as far away as the moon. I wanted to fly from California to Virginia Beach to see Fran. After her visit to Coronado Island my irritability increased with my lack of sleep. I hungered for the feel of her silky skin, and the sound of her clear, sweet voice. I needed to kiss her soft lips and drown in the warmth of those sparkling green eyes. She listened so intently as I entrusted her with many of my secret dreams and aspirations.

Because of the Navy cutbacks I had no choice but to book a flight on American Airlines for a trip to the East Coast. I packed a bag for myself and bought a crate for Boo-Dog so we could make the flight together. If Fran truly loved me as much as I thought she did she wouldn't object to my bringing my eighty-pound sheepdog to Virginia.

After we arrived, Fran curtailed her work hours over the weekend to spend as much time as possible with me. The weekend was wonderful for all of us. My dog and I spent hours on the beach, which was just across the street from Fran's home on 72nd Street. I enjoyed early morning runs with Boo-Dog and being away from the busy work schedule of the Warhawks in Lemoore. While I ran Fran would walk on the beach or relax and read until I returned. There were only a few tourists on the north end of the beach since most of the hotels were located further south toward Rudee Inlet Marina.

At night I relaxed and with each kiss Fran became more a part of me. I awakened in the morning and felt vibrantly alive with a renewed sense of belonging, an awareness of feeling complete. Fran was patient as she watched and waited for me to say my rowdy days were behind me. She could tell with every new story I took a personal risk of exposing more about myself. Either before or after an adventure I would submerge myself in the mysterious delight of Fran's welcoming body curled close beside me before we fell into a deep and contented sleep.

Fran was proud of her contemporary home located on the north end of Virginia Beach. She had been deeply involved in the design and construction, which had been completed just one year before we met. The weekend passed too quickly for both of us. In the late afternoon we walked together in Seashore State Park, which adjoined a corner of Fran's property, or we ventured down the block to the beach to watch the sunset and look out to sea.

Fran shared how she enjoyed sitting quietly on the beach gazing out across the large expanse of water. She daydreamed about what adventures awaited her in the future. She would watch dolphins leap into the air and splash back into the water and imagined what it would be like to experience such unrestricted freedom. She said, "I imagine carrier pilots with their undaunted daring and courage flying off of and landing aboard aircraft carriers are almost as free as the fish in the sea or the birds in the air, living life to its fullest."

Fran drifted into a story of her own, telling me how much she enjoyed living near the ocean. Deep sea fishing was a favorite activity. She had previously held a North Carolina record for catching a white marlin and another record for channel bass. Living near the beach she could see the fishing boats leaving and returning to Rudee Inlet Marina at the south end of the beach.

I could tell she found a great deal of peace just being close to the water. I said, "Boating definitely offers an opportunity to experience adventure and freedom. As a boy growing up near the Rogue River in Oregon my parents allowed me the freedom to explore the river. Some trips were with my father and sometimes I went alone. My favorite times were to follow the flow of the river a little further each trip. Boating may not be as exhilarating as a catapult shot but the experiences are still an exciting ride, providing hours of feeling vibrantly alive. You are rewarded with a myriad of challenges along with an enviable amount of thrills.

"Let me share another boating experience. However, tubing and canoeing brought plenty of thrills with friends. My good friend Gary Grosh owned an aluminum Grumman canoe we used to spend hours on the Rogue River challenging white water rapids. One occasion ended in a near tragedy. Hells Gate Canyon is a narrow stretch of the Rogue River where a fast-moving current is funneled into a more restricted canyon. The canyon is flanked on either side by rock walls that have been carved out by centuries of water flow. The walls are scalloped with large domes separated by cleavages that cause the rushing water to spin into high speed and deadly whirlpools. Gary was very skilled at maneuvering the canoe from the stern with me in the bow. On this trip the current overpowered his paddle when he attempted to center us once we entered the canyon. We were caught sideways at the most restricted point and the canoe capsized. It lodged against a rock under water."

"Gary and I were carried through the swirling canyon from one whirlpool to another. I know it sounds ludicrous now, but we never wore life jackets! We fought the whirlpools that moved us from one to another for over a half mile. We were pulled under water and thought we would drown. Fortunately we were both strong swimmers and, as we exited the canyon, although exhausted, we looked at one another and grinned. We had survived and would try the river on another day."

As I told the story I listened to her calm responses and thought how uniquely different our energies were. When we were together our differences didn't seem to matter. I realized Fran was energized by my enthusiasm for naval aviation, and I was equally captivated by the peaceful serenity of her world.

On Sunday we attended her church, and as I sat in the silence I felt tears roll down my cheeks in gratitude for this time in life to feel such peace. Just as Fran had been living her dream, so had I. Yet we had stumbled across another dream in a most unforeseen way, and I made a decision. I continued to sit quietly and experienced a new meaning of being afraid. *Afraid* was not ever seeing Fran again. I was also afraid of all the changes she represented, but the thought of being apart and not seeing her again was much more frightening.

In the afternoon we walked down to the beach. I turned to Fran and said, "I realize this is asking a lot, but would you consider moving to Lemoore? I love you and want us to have more time together before I go on cruise. I am aware your life was peaceful and organized before meeting me. Come fly with me, dream with me, and let me show you a whole new world. Every minute we are apart brings unfulfilled days. You have brought an entirely new dimension into my life. I am becoming a better man and without you I feel incomplete."

In a loving earnest voice she said, "My feelings for you are obvious to anyone who looks at us when we are together. Our cross-country courtship has become difficult for me, too. I had planned to go to Israel this summer with my class from Virginia Wesleyan College and work in a kibbutz. Let me talk to my daughters and hear what they want before leaving Virginia. Hopefully, Sherri and Sue will be excited to live close to their grandparents in California. The girls love spending time with them during the summer months. I have a buy-sell agreement on my business so that should not be an issue and my home is in a very desirable location and will sell quickly."

"However, we must talk. There are things in my past I buried like skeletons in a dark grave, and after five years of therapy I know who I am and what I want for my life. I am a strong woman, maybe the strongest you will ever come to know. Although God gave me the strength to survive an abusive childhood there are also areas of my life where I am vulnerable and at times fragile. Accepting me you have said that you will accept my daughters as your own. I know I will love your son Shane. He has a good mother and I will never attempt to take her place. Sherri and Sue know that they are loved. However, they have not been exposed to a loving relationship between a man and woman that they remember. You are opinionated and yet you are caring and gentle. In this area we will need to make adjustments because I have been overprotective of my daughters. Also, in loving me you accept the challenge of taking them through their teen years and into womanhood. I'm not sure that will be an easy task. I believe if anyone can do it you are that man.

I have failed at three relationships with men, if I count their father. Actually I shouldn't have said I failed at three because he gave me two wonderful daughters and I walked away from what was making me unhappy.

The hardest part to tell you is that we will never have a child together. At the age of twenty-five I had serious health issues which resulted in a total hysterectomy. I thought my heart would break when the man I loved left me."

"He said, 'I accept your daughters,' but added the caveat, 'every man needs a child of his own.' When that was not an option he left. Sherri and Sue don't remember much about him other than he made them eat food they didn't like. We were together for such a short time his leaving seemingly had little impact on them."

Bud my storyteller became Bud the sage, and could hear the pain behind my confession. He said. "Franny, I love you. I can't change your past, nor would I try. You are the woman sitting beside me who has walked through the ashes of despair and survived. I can't promise I will never cause you pain, but I will try to do my best to protect you. As far as the rest, we will have plenty of time to meld our lives together." Bud held me close as we sat quietly beside each other. The day came to a close with us lost in our thoughts about the future.

The decision was made and implementing the details of relocating went smoothly. Fran initiated the buy-sell agreement on her business in spite of the objection of her business partner. The beach home sold and settled within thirty days. I gained a new perspective of Fran and her management skills. I was reassured by her self-confidence and was optimistic about our future together.

Fran and her girls had an enjoyable drive cross-country. They arrived in Lemoore a day earlier than I expected. She dropped the girls off at their grandparents in Selma before continuing the thirty-mile drive to the naval base hoping to surprise me.

When she arrived at the VA-97 Warhawks hanger I was flying a test hop. She later told me, "Two handsome young lieutenants, Sheldon Otto and David Park, told me you would be landing soon. They asked me to climb into one of the jets sitting in the hanger bay and asked me to wait for them to bring you to me."

Fran waited for only a few minutes before she heard me asking why I needed to check out an aircraft tonight. I grumbled, "I'm done for the night and will take care of it tomorrow."

"No," they insisted, "this will only take a few minutes of your time."

"Alright," I reluctantly agreed, as I climbed up the ladder to take a look inside the cockpit of 307.

Our reunion was perfect and a wonderful way to begin our future together. We decided Fran and her daughters would stay in my tiny apartment with Boo-Dog until Fran purchased a home for us to live together as a family. The purchase of our new home went smoothly, and within two months Fran's furniture arrived from Virginia and the move into our new home was cause for celebration.

On several weekends I was able to spend time with my four-year-old son, Shane, and he became acquainted with his future big sisters Sherri and Sue. The girls would occasionally visit their grandparents, which gave Fran and me the privacy we were denied during the week. Late one night as Fran lay comfortably in my arms she turned to me and said, "Living in Virginia Beach I often wondered what adventure awaited me. Now I have the answer and no longer need to wonder. You are my adventure!"

As the relationship with *the woman worth pursuing* continued to mature, so did my memories of quality time spent with my son, Shane. When Shane was a baby I carried him in a backpack while mowing the lawn or visiting friends. The trio—Shane, Boo-Dog, and me—were inseparable. My yellow Jeep with no top, windshield down, Boo-Dog in the right seat and Shane in my lap, without a seat belt, could be seen all over town in Beaufort, South Carolina, and later in Montgomery, Alabama.

Cross-Country Courtship

After my tour with the Marines I received orders to the Air Force Command and Staff College at Maxwell Air Force Base in Montgomery, Alabama, where I concurrently received my master's degree in Guidance and Counseling. These memories would creep quietly into my mind and do battle with my newfound partner as we planned our future together.

16
Adjustments and Compromise

"Location is very important when buying a home," our real estate agent advised. He worked his magic and found us a home where several military families lived. The Trafton family lived across the street and became friends for life. Mary Trafton was raised in a large Navy family and married a Naval Academy officer following his graduation.

It was clear at the onset of our friendship that Mary knew all the rules and conduct necessary to become a part of this new world I had travelled three thousand miles to join. I'm sure her mother gave her a copy of *Service Etiquette* before she married to guide her through the trials of military life. Mary was lots of fun and a talented artist who enjoyed interior decorating. She also hosted lively, interesting dinner parties. As our friendship grew so did my appreciation and perspective of military life. I was the perfect student, although I doubt Mary considered me her *Navy wife-in-training*.

Her husband Will was also a Navy carrier pilot and a contemporary of Bud's. He was soft spoken, more intense than Bud, and was a marvelous father to their two sons. Mary was always thoughtful to introduce me to other Navy wives and from the very beginning of our friendship included Bud and me in her lively dinner parties. All of her parties would have a theme, which I found fascinating. I enjoyed helping her decorate for each occasion. If it was a Mexican theme then we had tablecloths in bold bright colors and dishes from across the border. Will and Mary had been stationed in Japan so they had dishes and accessories they had brought back to the states and used them at other parties.

As I watched I learned and gained experience, similar to what I had done for much of my life. I grew to enjoy almost every aspect of becoming a military wife. On one occasion Mary said, "Fran, learn the rules, and then if you break one you will know why you made the decision. Sometimes you break a rule in order to achieve the look you want to create." Mary and I had incredible energy and as soon as our men went to work and the children were off to school we would decorate, cook, share ideas and sometimes exchange furniture. I didn't just like this new lifestyle; I embraced it wholeheartedly. If I was in love before leaving Virginia, life was even better now. Sherri and Sue were happy living in a small town and Sue even made the junior high school cheerleader team. The whole experience only added to my happiness.

I recalled one of my journal entries where I had written: *I went to work during the summer in one of the local packinghouses in Kingsburg. I was once again assisting the farmers to harvest their crops. I was happy living with Mom Stella and obeying her rules. I did not mind the work and knew that I had a home to return to where I would have a delicious meal and a clean comfortable bed waiting for me. I would bathe and have clean clothes to put on in the evening. A girlfriend asked me, "Don't you just hate all the rules and restrictions Mom Stella imposes upon you?" I truly didn't comprehend what she was asking and the part I understood I was not willing to share with her. I liked the rules and restrictions. First, they told me Mom Stella cared about me, and second, I was learning how to conduct myself properly in society. Unconcerned, I went on my way wanting to do better and better to please Mom Stella.*

I really believed I could compromise and realized adjustments were a part of our developing relationship. Or, at least I believed that to be true. I readily acknowledged I needed order, systems and structure in my life. Learning new rules from my friend Mary and incorporating them into my personal vision worked well. As my vision expanded my skills improved.

One example of compromising was when I decided we needed more light in our foyer and realized that taking out the coat closet was a way to make it happen. Bud did not see it the same way. In fact, he couldn't see the difference

Adjustments and Compromise

at all. As far as he was concerned an architect had designed our floor plan and it was fine the way it was. Here is where adjustments can become an issue.

I kept thinking and talking about the foyer until Bud said, "Alright, do it, but only take the wall and closet halfway down. That will give you enough light." I compromised, and until the day we sold the house and moved I hated what I considered a half-assed result. There was light in the foyer when you opened the front door but you also saw the half wall that looked like a flight deck on an aircraft carrier. Our friend, George Dom, who later in his career commanded the Navy Blue Angel Flight Demonstration Team, bought the house when we were transferred and his realtor suggested he take the half wall out. Thank goodness because it was perfect and looked just like my vision. George's talented realtor later married Timothy Keating. With Wanda by his side, Tim became one of the most respected four star Admirals of our generation.

Another time came when I really thought I had compromised. Bud and I became interested in landscaping and gardening after noticing how nice our neighbor Ed Tetrick's yard looked. We took Ed's good counsel and the appearance of our lawn improved.

Next, we wanted a large flower bed on the side of the driveway. We hauled in dirt and named our flower bed *Orr Mountain*. We planted two evergreens and I selected perennials and annuals for planting. Bud hired a landscaper to put in a sprinkler system. The landscaper explained in detail what he thought would be the best system for us to use. He went through a long explanation of how plastic tubing to various plants was most efficient and cost effective. I wanted hard pipe with sprinkler heads that would pop up and gently spray my beautiful flowers.

I honestly thought I could let go, but after we went to bed and turned out the lights I lay there in the dark with my vision of the flower bed replaying over and over in my mind. I could also see what the landscaper had installed in my beautiful flower bed, over my silent objection. In the middle of the night I got out of bed and went outside in my night gown and ripped the despicable plastic tubing out of the ground. Bud came outside and cried, "Have you gone crazy? What are you doing?"

I said, "I want hard pipe with sprinklers that pop up and gently spray my pretty flowers."

He just looked at me. Shaking his head in bewilderment said, "Why didn't you just say so?" He put his arms around me and walked us back into the house.

I am so lucky! Now when we talk about the next move or the next house, Bud asks, "What are your plans?" He also tells anyone who cares to comment, "I love what Fran does, even when I don't understand what is coming next. She brings beauty into my life."

I established a reputation for renovating and redecorating within our community of friends. Some friends consider it obsessive or at least unusual that I decorate our home for each holiday. Friends often bring their friends over to show them what I have done to celebrate a season. After the holiday everything is put away neatly in clear plastic boxes to wait until their return the following year.

Bud made two requests after we moved in and were settled. I was happy to please him and compromise. First he said, "Let me get out of the bed in the morning before you start to make it, and second, I do not care how often you move furniture and redecorate. I just ask that once you have the bedroom decorated the way you want, do not move my bed again. I need to know where I am in the middle of the night if I wake up and need to pee."

I was accepted in this new community primarily because of Bud's charisma and popularity. At least that is what I thought in the beginning. At a Warhawks squadron party three women came up to me. Norma was the commanding officer's wife. She was beautiful, gregarious and the mother of five children. Helen Mary, the executive officer's wife, was generous to open her home regularly for squadron parties. Dottie was a good friend of Helen Mary's and I guess that was the reason she was at the Warhawks party. Anyway, the three of them came over and introduced themselves to me to make sure I was welcomed. Norma invited me to the next wives meeting, which I eagerly accepted. The memory of their walking across the room to meet me has stayed with me through the years.

First, they made me feel welcome, and I promised myself that in the future I would do the same thing to a new wife or girlfriend whose mate joined the squadron. Second, they commented on what I was wearing. My clothing was considered casual elegance, very East Coast, trendy with longer hemlines and more formal than what was being worn in the San Joaquin Valley of

Adjustments and Compromise

California. They said, "We like how you look and don't change for us." My lesson was that a in a Navy squadron, the men and women were from all parts of the United States with differing views, lifestyles and clothing. In this melting pot was a common thread of mutual support and love of Naval aviators.

It was late when we got home and going to bed was more appealing than sharing my thoughts about the squadron party. There would be time for us to talk in the morning.

Bud after his first solo in a T-2A Buckeye in Meridian, Mississippi, in 1966. John McCain was one of his instructors.

Bud in an A-4F Skyhawk on a *USS Enterprise* combat cruise with VA-113 in 1968.

VA-113 Stingers aboard the *USS Enterprise* in 1968.

Fran in Bermuda Naval Air Station following the death of Vice Admiral C.C. Smith in 1984.

Fran driving a Jeep Golden Eagle in Lemoore, California, while Bud was deployed in 1983.

Fran and Bud next to the *USS Enterprise* after their wedding onboard the ship in 1976.

Fran and Bud aboard the *USS Enterprise* with then-Captain C.C. Smith after their wedding.

Bud as Commanding Officer of VA-146 on the *USS Constellation* in 1982. (photo by Phan Rigg)

Bud after his VA-146 Change of Command in Lemoore, California, in 1983.

Fran in Virginia Beach, Virginia.

Bud and Larry Wahl, the first two Navy Exchange pilots with the first USMC Harrier squadron, shown here in China Lake, California.

Jew Collier hovering in his Harrier next to an iceberg in the North Atlantic near the polar ice cap in 1975. Photo taken by Bud while also hovering near the ice cap.

Bud and Fran backstage with Willie Nelson after Highway Men concert in Washington, D.C., in 1991.

F-14 Tomcats and FA-18 Hornets launching off of the *USS Constellation* in the Indian Ocean. Bud was the first senior (Super CAG) on the Connie.

"CAG" Bud piloting a B-1 Bomber out of McConnell AFB in 1989. Photo taken by "Shifty" Peairs in an FA-18 with "Trots" Trotter in the FA-18 on Bud's wing.

VA-122 A-7E Flying Eagle in Fallon, Nevada. Bud was Commanding Officer of the VA-122 Flying Eagles.

FA-18 "CAG Bird" over the *USS Constellation* in the Indian Ocean in 1988. Each of nine squadrons paint a "CAG Bird" with the Airwing colors and the Wing Commander's name on one of their aircraft.

Daughter Sue, Fran, and Bud after Bud flew into Miramar, California, from the *USS Constellation* after returning from cruise as "CAG 14" on *USS Constellation* in 1989.

"CAG" Bud preparing for a flight in the F-14 Tomcat with VF-21 on the *USS Constellation* in 1989.

Bud was greeted by his staff of the Presidential Commission on Women in Combat after his final flight in the Navy with the Blue Angels at Andrews AFB in 1992.

Christmas with friends in San Diego, California, 1987.

Bud and Fran's 30th Wedding Anniversary celebration in Visalia, California, in 1996.

Orr family reunion on Thanksgiving 2008 in Mooney Park, Visalia, California.

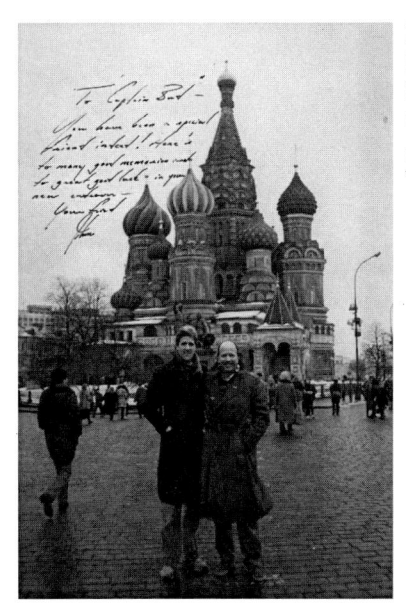

Bud with Senator John Kerry in Moscow in 1992. They were investigating the possibility of U.S. POWs who may have been moved into Russia during the Vietnam Conflict.

Bud with Senator John McCain in Hanoi. The statue is in honor of the North Vietnamese "gunners" who shot McCain down in 1967. He parachuted into the lake shown behind the statue. Photo taken in 1991.

17
One Night—Two Strikes

I worked out regularly. I awakened early and realized I hadn't run for a couple of days. I rolled over in bed, my eyes thick with sleep, and ran my hands over Fran's soft, smooth skin. I thought, "Dammit, this is the reason I haven't been running. Lying here with Fran in my arms makes me want to forget about running and instead spend the morning tangled up in the sheets. If I keep this up the next time I need to pull a few extra g's I'm going to wish I had gone for a run."

"Fran, how do you stay so trim?" I asked.

"Maybe it's my metabolism. I have always been active. Participating in my young daughter's activities, running a successful business and maintaining a home, I get plenty of exercise," she laughed.

"Do you have gym shoes?"

"Of course, when I lived in Virginia Beach I enjoyed going for long walks on the beach or exploring Seashore State Park."

"Let's go for a run," I said, and patted Fran's firm, smooth ass. Touching her and the shock of pleasure I received made me reconsider leaving the bed. The view was very pleasant from where I lay. Instead I pulled on a pair of workout shorts and left the room to feed Boo-Dog while Fran dressed for the run.

When I returned to the bedroom the door was open. I looked at Fran and stared. She was wearing a baby pink gym suit with white trim and little pink bows on her white tennis shoes. Her long golden brown hair was pulled up into a pony tail, tied with a pink ribbon. *WTFO!* ("What the fuck over" one of my more common aviator phrases.) I had on Australian split running shorts, New Balance gym shoes and a tee shirt with the squadron logo on the back. I shook my head and grinned, "Damn, she looks awfully cute but can that filly run?"

Fran's innocent expression and twinkle in her delicious green eyes seemed to say, "You lead. I'll be your wingman."

Less than a mile into my three-mile run, Fran asked me to go ahead and she would follow at her own pace. "When I see you returning I'll take the lead," she announced happily.

Fran turned homeward when she saw me running toward her. We ran together for the remainder of the run and cooled down on the front lawn. I went inside and grabbed a beer for myself and a bottle of water for Fran.

"Tell me the truth," I asked, "was that your first run?"

Fran answered with a saucy, easy smile, "Let's do it again tomorrow."

That night I took Fran out to the flight line and the LSO platform so she could watch *touch and go* field carrier landing practice. She had a ringside seat and seemed thrilled to watch each pilot fly several simulated night carrier landings. I sat beside her, only a few feet from the runway. Fran wore one of my olive drab green flight suits and a headset I had given her to wear to protect her ears. She looked adorable in the baggy flight suit, so small, vulnerable and fragile.

Fran looked up at me and said, "To be in the presence of so much masculinity is over-whelming. The scent is a combination of tangy deodorant and jet fuel. I find it to be a sexy, desirable smell."

On the way home Fran asked, "Are all LSOs as qualified and experienced as you?"

"Let me tell you a story and you draw your own conclusion."

During my tour in VA-122 Flying Eagles Replacement Air Group, I was an instructor pilot and also the senior landing signal officer (LSO). There were two RAG squadrons at Naval Air Station Lemoore. The VA-125 Rough Raiders flew the A-7B Corsair II and my squadron, the VA-122 Flying Eagles, flew the A-7E Corsair II.

The A-7E was more sophisticated than the A-7B. The Ling Temco Vought A-7E also had a completely different engine than the A-7B and required a totally different training syllabus. This necessitated the need for two Replacement Air Group squadrons.

The LSO of each Replacement Air Group (RAG) class watched as his pilots completed the required field carrier landing practice (FCLP) day and night at the naval air station. After completing training they were ready to carrier qualify aboard the *USS Hancock*. The *USS Hancock* had been decommissioned shortly after World War II. In the early 1950s she was modernized and re-commissioned as an attack aircraft carrier. In her second career she operated exclusively in the Western Pacific arena, playing a prominent role in the Vietnam War. The *Hancock* had a much smaller flight deck than the super aircraft carriers, *USS Enterprise, USS Ranger,* and the *USS Kitty Hawk*. The smaller flight deck presented additional challenges for the RAG classes.

The final requirement for each class of pilots to graduate was flying aircraft they would inevitably fly in the fleet and most likely in combat. Each student was required to achieve ten day carrier landings and six night landings to qualify. After qualifying, the pilots would be ready to go to their assigned fleet squadron and respective carrier airwing aboard associated aircraft carriers. Most pilots would be headed to the Tonkin Gulf to fly combat missions in Vietnam.

Once the sun set and the first day of carrier qualifications was completed, the night carrier qualifications began. VFP-63 pilots, flying the F-8 Crusaders, were scheduled to land first. The Crusader was known to be the most difficult and challenging fleet aircraft to land aboard an aircraft carrier.

The landing signal officer for the Crusaders was a rugged looking, older Lieutenant Commander who had flown F-8 Crusaders for many years. His call sign was Hamm.

The A-7E looked like a fat version of the Crusader. When taking off and landing, the sleek, supersonic Crusader looked as if the wing would rise up. In actuality, when slowing to approach air speed the fuselage lowered and the wing stayed constant. Because of the long fuselage and high nose attitude or angle of attack the pilot could not see over the nose when landing aboard the aircraft carrier. The engineers designed the wing to be extended by a large hydraulic actuator. The actuator was manually selected by the pilot as part of the landing checklist along with the landing gear, flaps, and tailhook. The wing appeared to ascend. However, what happened was the nose of the aircraft would lower, allowing the pilot to see his intended point of landing over the nose of the aircraft.

As night flight operations began, the head landing signal officer (LSO) of each RAG class was on the platform. Hamm was prepared to wave his class of F-8 Crusaders who were on final approach to the aircraft carrier. The Crusaders descended from the holding pattern at one-minute intervals. They were picked up on radar and vectored in by a carrier-controlled approach to a point three-quarter of a mile behind the ship. The Air Traffic Controller advised the first pilot, "Crusader 105 you are at three-quarter mile, call the ball."

Now the pilot switched his scan from instruments to visual, and looked out at the aircraft carrier for the first time. All a pilot could see were the white lights that outlined the aircraft carrier's landing area and the strobing white centerline lights. The red drop lights were mounted on the center of the stern of the carrier from the flight deck to the waterline. The red drop line light gave the appearance of being an extension of the centerline when a pilot was lined up properly. If the pilot wasn't lined up properly what he saw was an arrow formed by the strobing white centerline lights on the flight deck and the red drop line lights pointing in the direction he needed to turn to line up on centerline.

The Fresnel lens was mounted on the port side of the ship behind the LSO platform, and consisted of a series of square yellow block lights stacked on top of each other. The refraction was so finite that at any given time a pilot would see only one cell at a time. The relationship of the yellow *meatball* light in the center of the lens to the green datum lights on either side told a pilot if he was high or low relative to the glide slope. Ideally the pilot would see only the yellow *meatball* light centered between the green rows of lights. A pilot was constantly adjusting the aircraft's power and nose attitude to bring the *meatball* to the center of the green lights from either below or above them.

One Night—Two Strikes

When a pilot landed aboard the carrier with the yellow ball between the green datum lights he would in most instances engage the number three arresting gear wire, the *target wire*. When a pilot was high he might catch the four wire or possibly miss all the wires and *bolter*. Should he *bolter* and miss all the wires he would be picked up by the radar controller and vectored around by radar to make another approach to the aircraft carrier.

The yellow ball below the green lights meant the pilot was below glide path and would land short of the number three arresting gear wire and engage the number one or two arresting gear wire. If the aircraft was really low the pilot would see the bottom cell of the Fresnel lens which was red and pulsating. Should the aircraft continued on this flight path it most likely would land short of the flight deck. The landing gear or even the fuselage of the aircraft would crash into the stern of the ship, causing the pilot to eject from his aircraft or die.

The F-8 Crusader's stubby wings and long fuselage made lateral corrections for line-up appear jerky and quick. Inside the aircraft, at three-quarters of a mile from the aircraft carrier, things happened very quickly and Hamm was alert to any change in engine power or nose attitude. The change in engine power could be detected by the sound of the engine; the attitude change (the up or down movement of the nose) would be observed by the approach lights changing on the aircraft.

The first two Crusaders landed safely at night aboard the aircraft carrier and the pilots received satisfactory grades from Hamm. As the number three F-8 arrived at the three-quarter mile position to call the ball, Hamm detected fear in the pilot's voice as he made the call, "103 Crusader ball." The pilot continued to jockey the throttle up and down causing the jet engine to whine at varying frequencies.

Every landing signal officer on the platform was frozen into silence as Hamm used a soothing, yet commanding voice to calm the pilot, direct him back to the glide path and smooth out his throttle movements. The Crusader was a little high as the aircraft crossed the ramp. Once the pilot realized his aircraft was high he stuffed the nose toward the flight deck. At the same time he pulled the power back in a futile attempt to catch one of the arresting gear wires. The aircraft dove toward the stern of the ship and impacted the ramp in front of the aircraft's main landing gear.

Hamm screamed, "Eject! Eject!" The pilot screeched by in what was left of his Crusader. The canopy blew off and the explosion of the Martin Baker ejection seat with the pilot strapped in by his torso harness shot high into the sky. The parachute opened, and the pilot descended ahead of the ship and toward the sea.

The rear half of the aircraft broke off and crashed into the ocean while the cockpit and nose of the aircraft careened down the deck, engulfed in flames. The huge ensuing explosion caused burning fuel to burst high into the sky over the flight deck.

The rescue of the pilot and the careening piece of aircraft was forgotten as everyone on the LSO platform dove into the escape net off the port side of the aircraft carrier. Most of us were certain we were going to die. Bodies were piled in on top of one another as a cloud the burning jet fuel and debris rained down on us.

When it was safe to crawl out of the escape net, we made our way back to the flight deck to observe the search and rescue helicopter overhead trying to find the pilot in the water. The Captain of the ship had ordered an immediate hard turn to starboard in order for the carrier to avoid running over the pilot in the water. Thankfully he was rescued safely, the flight deck was cleared, and the *USS Hancock* returned to flight operations.

The next class to begin night landings were the A7-Bs from VA-125 Rough Raiders. My class from VA-122 Flying Eagles would be the last event of the night. The first few pilots flying the A-7B Corsairs flew aboard the carrier and received satisfactory night landing grades. Next in the groove was Lieutenant Junior Grade Jack Bushwash. At three-quarters of a mile Bushwash was handed off by the Air Traffic Controller to Gerry, the landing signal officer who said, "You are at three-quarter mile, call the ball." This meant the pilot had visual contact with the aircraft carrier.

Lieutenant Bushwash keyed the mike and made the call, "403 Corsair ball, state four point eight."

Gerry said, "Roger, ball, you're a little high." This meant 403 was a little above glide slope. Regrettably, Bushwash did not respond to Gerry's call and maintained his approach above the three-degree glide slope. Every LSO on the platform could tell by the pilot's voice that he was in extreme cockpit overload.

"Bud, what do you mean the pilot was in cockpit overload?" Fran asked.

"Haven't you had days when you think to yourself that you can't deal with one more issue? By the tone in Bushwash's voice we knew he wasn't coping with the multiple tasks required for him to get aboard the carrier."

From my position on the LSO platform I watched Bushwash's aircraft drift to the right of centerline. At the same time Gerry concentrated on the aircraft's high approach and continued to talk the pilot down without realizing the aircraft was drifting further to the right of centerline.

"Was the pilot in danger because he was drifting to the right?" Fran asked.

"Stay with me, Fran, and I'll tell you."

Finally 403 arrived at the ramp, high and lined up right. In retrospect, Gerry should have given the pilot a wave-off. However, he called, "Left for line up and fly it down."

"Ouch!" A left for line up call was almost always a bad call, especially when the aircraft was in close to the ramp. The reason was a pilot would not have time to counter the momentum caused by a last quick bank to the left and would land drifting right to left toward the portside of the carrier.

"Why was it so dangerous?" Fran wanted to know.

"A carrier landing is very precise, especially in close to the ship. If the pilot is too high or too low, or not lined up correctly within a certain point and attempts to correct, the result is usually catastrophic."

In addition to the *fly it down* call, Bushwash realized he was too high. He stuffed the nose down and at the same time banked hard to the left. The aircraft landed hard and engaged the number two wire. Lieutenant junior grade Bushwash pushed the engine to full power as was always done as soon as you land aboard the aircraft carrier. In the event a pilot missed all of the wires and *boltered,* the jet engine was spooled up to full power in time for the aircraft to fly safely away from the angle deck.

As the Corsair slammed down on the flight deck it continued a right to left drift and traveled all the way to the edge of the flight deck. The heavy jarring impact of the aircraft brought it to a violent a stop at full power. The A7-B was held in place by the fully extended arresting gear wire and the port main mount off the side of the ship. The aircraft only stayed there for several seconds before it began to roll slowly to the left, at which time Bushwash initiated ejection. The canopy blew off, the ejection seat rocket fired and shot the pilot straight out at ninety degrees, skipping across the ocean, into the dark night. Later we would find it hard to believe that the pilot was safely rescued.

Incredibly, the aircraft did not fall into the ocean. The power was still at one hundred percent and a triangle of thrust was formed by the arresting gear hook holding the aircraft from going forward and hanging by the starboard main mount while the wheel remained stuck in the scupper, the small railing that runs along the side of the ship.

On the LSO platform we were peering around the jet blast deflector that protected us from jet blast. We were looking right up the tailpipe of the fuselage of the engine with full power blasting right at us. The noise was so loud that we could not hear the radios. The crash crew raced out to the front of the aircraft in a starter cart, pointed a long nozzle down the intake and shot foam into the engine. The injection of foam quickly extinguished the engine. By shutting the engine down the triangle of tension that was holding the jet onto the flight deck and hanging by the Corsair's starboard landing gear released. Once the thrust from the engine was gone, the aircraft continued a roll to port and fell toward the sea nose down. From the platform we watched this incredible sight and expected to see a big splash as the aircraft with no pilot or canopy crashed into the ocean, right beside the carrier. That didn't happen!

The aircraft stopped with the nose about fifteen feet off the water, dangling awkwardly by the tailhook, still attached to the number two arresting gear wire. An alert, quick-thinking Air Boss and flight deck crew dispatched a team of yellow shirts out to the side of the ship. The yellow shirts cut several of the bolts that attached the Cross Deck Pendent (CDP) to the arresting gear cable and weakened several more. A courageous yellow shirt driver who worked on the flight deck got into a starter cart with a miniature tailhook attached to the back of the cart. He hooked the tailhook over the arresting gear wire, and pulled a life jacket up over his head and back to protect him from a recoiling CDP. He stomped on the gas and broke the remaining bolts. The bolts sheared the CDP from the carrier flight deck and allowed whatever was remaining of the Corsair to crash into the sea below the deck.

After the pilot was safely rescued with a crushed shoulder the yellow shirts on the flight deck did a quick foreign object damage walk down. It was important to make sure the landing area was free from debris left by the crash landing. Within minutes of the all clear signal the Air Boss came up on the loud speaker on the flight deck and announced, "Land aircraft."

"Holy crap," I said. "Two crashes in one night and now it was my turn to land my guys safely aboard the carrier."

Fortunately, the rest of the night went without further catastrophe. My class did well, and I retired to the dirty shirt wardroom for coffee and sliders (the greasy cheeseburgers) served after late-night flight operations. The back of my white LSO jersey and green camies were covered, as they always were after flight operations, with the heavy grease from snapping retracting arresting gear wires.

At 1:00 in the morning I went up to the ship's radio compartment to wait my turn to get on the radio. At the conclusion of every flight operation cycle the senior LSO from each detachment was required to radio back to his home base and report the results of day and night operations aboard the aircraft carrier. As I waited my turn, a young man came out of the radio room wearing a blue hospital robe with a Navy Medical Corps insignia on it. Since I didn't recognize the man I asked, "Hey, are you the guy who punched out of the Crusader tonight?"

"Yeaaah, that was me!"

"How was that?"

To my amazement the young pilot said, "Just like the last time. I just got off the radio with my wife. After the last time I ejected, I promised her if I ever ejected again I would quit. I'm done!"

Man, I would never want to be in that guy's place.

18
Second Thoughts

Bud appeared happy and pleased with the transition from bachelorhood to family life. Amid my planning for a small garden wedding in our backyard I felt the universe tilt slightly on its axis. I approved our wedding invitations, began addressing them and made arrangements for our wedding reception at the Lemoore Officer's Club. Bud and I agreed to delay our honeymoon until I could join him in the Philippines midway through his next six-month cruise. CAUTION! Everything only appeared to move along smoothly as the earth moved and the universe continued its tilt.

Bud was having second thoughts, which I recognized as he began stopping by the Officer's Club before coming home in the evening. I had known instinctually he was not a man who could be kept on too tight a leash. One weekend when the girls were visiting their grandparents, I asked him if he was ready to share whatever was troubling him. He searched my expectant green eyes and said, "I don't know what's causing my confusion. You have the promise of my love but I am not ready to make a lifetime commitment. Please try and understand, I was the cause of my first marriage failing. A good woman gave up on me and my self-destructive behavior, not just my antics while with the Marines but other times as well. But more important, I have not come to terms with being unable to raise my son. I don't want to hurt you, but I can't get married right now."

"Oh no!" was all I could think at the time. I cried, but I did it privately. I was even positive Bud shed a tear or two. I am inherently a private person but have trained myself to be socially outgoing. But not now—I let Bud know I did not want or desire company from anyone in the squadron. Trying hard to keep myself under control I quietly said, "Life happens. I have faced heartbreak in my life, and I promise you I will survive."

I was grateful that our wedding invitations had not been mailed. When I could speak I said, "Of course we will postpone our wedding since you are not ready to make a commitment. Please pack your bags and move into the Bachelor Officer Quarters on base. You are scheduled to leave on cruise in two months and then you will be gone for six months."

After Bud's bags were packed and he was ready to leave I said, "I love you and pray you will change your mind or at the very least make a decision before you leave on cruise." I was wise enough not to push him in either direction.

Once I was alone I thought back to an earlier time in my life when I unfortunately attempted to build a life on the wrong foundation. I had written in my journal: *My mother, the wandering nomad is off again in search of a new horizon. I shared my difficult situation with Doug, the serious, naive boy I dated. He listened amazed and then sympathetic as I expressed my disappointment over my mother abandoning my brother and I again. I had run out of places to live. The homes of girlfriends were only temporary shelters until I could relocate. I was also positive that my father would not have a place for me.*

Doug was obedient and respectful to his parents, whom I found extremely proper and well educated in comparison to my family. His mother had been a school teacher and his father owned a family business. Doug was a freshman at Reedley Junior College with plans to follow in his mother's footsteps and become a schoolteacher.

One afternoon I stopped by Doug's home to see if he had heard the news that Buddy Holly, a popular singer, had been killed in a plane crash. It was also a chance for me to meet his parents. Our worlds were so different. I admired everything about his Scandinavian parents and the attractive, clean neighborhood where they lived. I saw the order and stability of their life and wanted to someday live that way.

They were pleasant to me, but stood back knowing I wasn't "their kind." If they had known my future plans for their youngest son, they would have barred me from entering the doorway. I had seen enough of the manipulative techniques of women to attain their heart's desire to believe I could convince Doug to help me find a way to stay in Selma and graduate from high school. I knew that by completing high school my dream of becoming a self-sufficient person was possible, so graduation was tantamount to my survival.

On Sunday afternoon Doug offered to take me for a ride. On the way home I learned where couples in high school went to make out and be alone. Selma, The Raisin Capital of the World—if you believe the signage coming into and going out of town—has rows and rows of vineyards with wide, flat, even rows. The rows were wide enough for a car to drive through.

The boy who first figured out what a great place the vineyards were to park must have become a local high school hero. Privacy is precious to any teenager. I never asked Doug how he knew where to go or if he was sure we would be alone. After he parked his car he opened his arms and I willingly entered his embrace. It was an exciting experience as his lips increased their pressure and the kisses deepened. I allowed myself to feel the pleasure of increased intimacy with someone I trusted and someone who cared for me. I felt cherished, special and wanted. The gentle tenderness Doug expressed was the beginning of my knowledge that the human body can heal from whatever pain it has endured once it allows the heart to open up. That night as I lay awake in my bed I realized I was happy and felt optimistic about the future.

Doug decided to quit college and join the Army Reserves in order for us to be married immediately. His six months of active duty would be his first real job. We were like two children playing house in the simplistic analysis we made regarding our future. I borrowed a dress from a girlfriend to wear to our wedding. My mother acted as Doug's witness on our wedding license and pretended to be his mother. My grandmother signed as my witness.

I had one final talk with my mother prior to the wedding ceremony. I asked, "How I can I prevent myself from becoming pregnant?"

She casually shrugged me off by saying, "Men take care of that sort of thing." Perhaps she was right and men knew where and how to purchase contraceptives. Also, if she was right and men took care of that sort of thing, how did she end up having five children? She overlooked the fact that I was marrying a boy who was inexperienced sexually instead of the worldly men she knew. With all my exposure to sex I remained ignorant as to who should take responsibility for the prevention of making babies. At the time we were both too embarrassed to talk to each other about the subject. We also knew how hard it was to keep a secret in a small town, so we did not discuss the subject with anyone other than my family. We were afraid if anyone knew what we were planning his parents might find out and not allow Doug to marry me.

After the simple ceremony we said good-bye to my family and drove the thirty miles to Fresno. We had enough money between us for a simple dinner and a motel room. We were two scared children holding our marriage license as we checked into the motel. We called mother to tell her where we were staying. We drew comfort and security from the official certificate and the fact that we could sleep together.

We were surprised to be awakened early the next morning with a loud knock on our door and the arrival of Doug's parents. Mother had called to inform them of our marriage and where we were staying in Fresno. They were shocked and disappointed at the outrageous behavior of their normally obedient son.

We returned to Selma with Doug's parents following us in their car. They had Doug drop me off at my house before he drove to his home. Doug kissed me good-bye on my front porch and said, "Try not to worry. I will return as soon as I can." They told Doug that we would remain separated until the decision was made as to whether our marriage would be accepted by his family or if it would be annulled.

I didn't hear from anyone for the remainder of the day or throughout the night. The next morning I dressed and went to school. Perhaps this seemed like a strange thing to do but I didn't want to miss school and I didn't know when I would see Doug again. The kids were shocked that I came to school, but to me it didn't seem unusual. I was determined to graduate from high school.

I was sent home from school by my guidance counselor and told to wait for Doug's mother to pick me up. She controlled her emotions as she asked me to get into the car and drove me to her beautiful home. Once inside the home she asked me to sit down on the sofa and listen very carefully to her. She began to cover the rules I would need to obey in order to become a member of their family. I was to come live with them and finish high school. I was to disassociate myself from further contact with "my people." I kept waiting for her to explain the hard part, but it never came. It was very easy for me to agree to her demands. She didn't seem to understand my alternatives. Doug was to leave over the weekend for Fort Ord, California, to serve six months of active duty in the Army. I, the obedient child, climbed into a clean, soft bed with crisp white sheets, which smelled like Ivory soap, for the first time in a very long time.

Second Thoughts

Within the short span of a few years, I totally divorced myself from the culture of my early childhood. I learned the art of managing a home, including how to keep it clean, set a table, and provide my family with well-balanced meals. I gave birth to two beautiful baby girls, taught Sunday School at the First Baptist Church and in the evenings I read books or sewed clothing for myself and my two little girls.

Doug and I had come together for different reasons and would not remain married. I experienced the depth of his mother's love for her grandchildren when I told her I was leaving her son. She had helped us purchase the home next door and had seen her grandchildren every day of their lives. The news was heartbreaking to her. She said, "Doug can leave, but I want you and the girls to stay in your home." I reminded her of what she had said right after Doug and I were married.

My brother had joined the Air Force, and one night leaving the base he had been involved in an automobile accident. Someone in the family called to say he was okay but his baby was seriously injured. I wanted to go to see him. Doug's mother said, "This is what I was afraid of, blood will always win. Fran, the only way you can change the direction of your future is to deny your past." I listened to her words and the decision was a difficult one to make. In the end I did what she asked.

Had I returned to "my people" in the early stages of my relationship with Doug and his family I do not think I would have been able to keep the pieces of my life together. I knew instinctively I was fragile and would not be able to deal with the reoccurrence of family traumas without it impacting my life in a negative way.

Although my marriage ended in divorce, I had not failed completely. I left the marriage with two beautiful daughters and several years of invaluable strict discipline and training. I continued to maintain contact with Doug's parents because I believed that through them the opportunity existed for my daughters to have a stable childhood. I knew they would be taught to value their Scandinavian heritage. Once again it was if I had no past, as if it had never existed and was never mentioned.

My daughters, Sherri and Sue, brought meaning and purpose to my life. With them I was in harmony with the natural flow of my existence. I loved their sweet innocence and wanted to make sure they grew up in an environment that would promote their potential. I promised God I would be a good mother and always be there for them. He knew I would never abandon them and would try to provide them a better life than I had been able to attain.

I was back in the world on my own, totally responsible for not only myself but also two young daughters. The added responsibilities did not bother me because I had been freed of what brought me unhappiness. I escaped from my past by getting married. Now, I made my escape from marriage, seeking happiness, to avoid a life that was barren of fulfillment as a woman.

I didn't pretend that Bud changing his mind was just another bump in the road. However, I was sensitive to all the changes he had experienced in the past year. The year before meeting me had been painful and caused him to be afraid of starting a new relationship with a ready-made family. I had time to realize what would happen in the future between Bud and me was not in my control. I was not willing to manipulate him into returning to me before he was ready.

Fortunately we both wanted to stay in contact after he left. Bud found the courage to ask me to go to San Francisco with him the weekend before the airwing. went aboard the *Enterprise* and departed on cruise. David Park, Bud's roommate aboard the aircraft carrier and squadron mate in VA-97 Warhawks, and his wife Rita encouraged me to join Bud for the weekend.

David said, "We realize how delicate your relationship with Bud is right now. He is miserable without you, but he just can't make a commitment. Please consider going to San Francisco with him. We don't think you would be compromising yourself if you go and say good-bye before the airwing leaves on our six-month cruise."

19
A Nuclear Carrier Wedding

Fran called me after David and Rita left and asked, "What time should I pick you up for the trip to San Francisco?" As I got into her car my first thought was how happy I was to hold her again in my arms. I tried to explain my reluctance, but Fran shushed me with a finger to my lips and quietly said, "It's alright, I know you love me and that is enough for now. I love you and know you must find the answer you are searching for and what you want for your future. I can accept your reluctance to marry, even though you're unsure why you're holding back. Whatever the future holds will be for the best. I will pray you and the airwing have a safe cruise. I am certain a decision will be made one way or the other before you return to Lemoore."

"Where did this unshakeable woman come from?" I asked my Censor, not expecting an answer.

Fran watched the *Enterprise* with me aboard sail under the Golden Gate Bridge before returning to Lemoore and an uncertain future. Saying farewell to her in San Francisco proved more painful than all of our previous good-byes combined. This time was different. A decision needed to be made, but that had not happened. Once again, I saw Fran's strength and determination when she said, "I will give you time to make up your mind as to whether you want me in your life. We will not live together unless we are married. If you cannot decide, I will make plans to return to my life and career in Virginia Beach."

I stood on the bow of the *Enterprise* as the aircraft carrier passed under the Golden Gate Bridge. Small pebbles from the bridge rained down upon my head. The pebbles seemed to say, "Stupid, stupid, stupid."

"My God, what the hell have I done? What if Fran meets someone else before I make a decision? I pray she knows I love her, but if I repeat my outrageous behavior with her I am not sure I would recover. Failure is too frightening to think about," I anguished over and over. On a mystical level I felt Fran understood my thoughts and that was one of the reasons she opened her arms and let me go.

The *USS Enterprise* sailed into the Western Pacific with the first port visit being Hawaii. I left the ship and headed for the Officer's Club feeling unsettled and miserable. I drank a few beers, hoping to drown my confusion and unhappiness. I danced with the girls in the bar until I happened to look up and see a woman across the room who caused my heart to skip a beat. "Is that Fran?" I asked. After realizing my mistake I drank a few more beers to numb my body and headed back to the ship. I told my Commanding Officer I would take duty for anyone who wanted to go ashore during the remainder of the port of call. I chose to stay aboard the ship until the *Enterprise* sailed toward the Philippines.

After the *USS Enterprise* was underway I went up to the bridge to visit Captain Smith. I wanted to continue my training to become a conning officer who would assist the ship's company during underway replenishment at sea. Captain Smith and I had become friends in Coronado in spite of our rank differential. The Captain had enjoyed meeting Fran in San Diego during the Coronado Island port visit and festivities. He had said, "She will be a challenge but I think she is perfect for you."

One look at me and his suspicions where confirmed. "Bud, what are you going to do about Fran?" Captain Smith asked.

"How do I know if I have changed my behavior and my feelings for Fran will last? She is the most fascinating woman I had ever met, but she won't settle for less than marriage. You know I failed miserably at my first marriage. What makes me think I would do differently a second time? I screwed up royally and the mother of my child moved on with her life without me. Maybe I'm not monogamous."

A Nuclear Carrier Wedding

"Bud," said Captain Smith in his slow, deep, southern voice, "It seems pretty simple to me, what you need to do is make a decision and make it right."

After leaving Hawaii the *USS Enterprise* steamed into the Philippines for a port visit and to take on supplies. It was also an opportunity during the next few days for pilots to fly bombing practice. I had an early flight at the airfield in Cubi Point, Philippines, with the Executive Officer (XO) of the *Enterprise*, Barney Kelly. (Commander Kelly would later in his career become a four-star Admiral and Commander of the Pacific Fleet in Hawaii.) Barney and I briefed before flying to a target located on a small rock island reserved for bombing practice.

Before our flight I was greeted by two Marine Harrier pilots from my old VMA-513 Flying Nightmares squadron who were deployed to the Philippines. The pilots exchanged the usual, "who knew who and do you know where so and so is stationed?" The Harrier pilots invited me to fly one of the AV-8A Harriers.

I quickly replied, "Hell no! That aircraft tried to kill me on more than one occasion and didn't succeed. I promise you I'm not going to let it have another opportunity."

After Barney and I finished bombing practice and landed back aboard the air station we returned to the Warhawks' ready room aboard the aircraft carrier. We were drinking iced tea when a call came over the squawk box, "Lieutenant Commander Orr, you have a call from the states in the Operations Office." I excused myself and climbed the ladder to the 0-3 level and walked into the Operations Office.

I picked up the phone and said, "Lieutenant Commander Orr."

The voice on the other end said, "When are you going to marry me?!"

When I retell the story I often joke and say my answer was, "Who is this?" But in reality I knew who it was, *the woman worth pursuing* and the woman I wanted to commit my love.

Before I could stammer out an answer, Fran continued, "You have thirty days to make up your mind or I'm moving back to Virginia Beach to resume my career."

I answered, "I understand and promise to get back to you very soon. Fran, you know I love you."

"I know you do, and you have my terms."

The *Enterprise* left the Philippines after the port call and sailed toward Hobart, Tasmania, just off the coast of Southern Australia. Hobart was the state capital and most populous city of the Australian island state of Tasmania. I found it interesting that it was founded as a penal colony. Hobart was Australia's second oldest capital city after Sydney.

In port most of us boys had a hard night of drinking in town. The Australians loved the U.S. military presence. There was an unprecedented patriotic remembrance of how the United States helped the Australians in World War II. The World War II Australian veterans wore parts of their uniform and medals and traded medals with U.S. sailors. The people in town invited the sailors into their homes for meals and the young women *devoured them*.

Once underway, I took my first opportunity to meet with Captain Smith on the bridge. I knew the Captain cared for Fran and always gave me sound advice. This time was no exception.

Captain Smith asked, "Bud what are you waiting for? The Philippines would be a perfect place for a wedding. Don't you want to marry Fran?"

Perhaps that was the question I needed to hear and said, "Of course I want to marry her."

We agreed that I should invite Fran to the Philippines during our port visit over the Thanksgiving holiday. The November holiday was also the fifteenth anniversary of the *Enterprise*, America's first nuclear carrier. The wedding would be held on the fo'c'sle of the famous aircraft carrier. The fo'c'sle, or forecastle, was the forward upper part of the bow below the flight deck and on the *Enterprise* was a large, pristine, white anchor room. Furthermore, Captain Smith, in true southern gentlemen form, asked, "Bud, may I have the honor of walking Fran down the aisle and giving the bride away?"

I laughed, "Hot damn! Everyone wins!"

Before leaving port in Hobart I called Fran, took a deep breath and calmly said, "The ship will pull into the Philippines in thirty days. Why don't you join me and bring a wedding gown?"

I arrived at the Manila International Airport in the Philippines carrying a long, satin champagne-colored wedding gown. It was unreasonably hot and

A Nuclear Carrier Wedding

humid inside the airport where total chaos reigned inside and out. David and Bud were forced to wait outside the terminal for David's wife Rita and me to pass through customs.

When we walked outside the terminal building I spotted Bud and immediately ran into his welcoming arms. It seemed as if only a minute passed for the kisses to deepen to a point where neither one of us wanted to stop. David tapped Bud on the shoulder and reminded him we were running late to complete the paperwork the Philippine government required for our marriage ceremony. Rita had flown into the Philippines with me and would be my maid-of-honor. David would be Bud's best man. The rules and regulations of an American serviceman getting married overseas had a strict protocol and Bud and I would not have a moment alone for the remainder of the day in order to complete all of the necessary forms.

I was exhausted from the long tiring flight, the heat and all the demands to finish the administrative tasks. Arriving at the Bachelor Officer Quarters Bud suggested I take a shower and relax and he would bring us something cold to drink. The squadron planned to meet at the Cubi Officers' Club for dinner. There was always an air of excitement when the ship pulled into port. Several wives and girlfriends from the airwing had traveled from the states to join their husbands or boyfriends for the long-awaited port visit. The magnificent fraternity of the airmen had a long-standing ritual of being together the first night in port.

When I returned to the room Fran was wrapped in a white terry cloth robe and lay on the bed asleep. I didn't have the heart to wake her and instead stood and looked at her feminine form resting peacefully. I allowed the tears to roll down my cheeks as I prayed, "Dear God, don't let me fuck this up."

Fran awakened with me lying beside her. She looked down at my lean, athletic body and noticed I was thinner than when I left on cruise. She smiled, "You are the love I have waited for. I promise to be your partner for the rest of my life."

I loved this woman who looked at me with such happiness shining in her eyes and pulled her into my arms to savor the sweet delicious taste of her mouth. I realized we had been given a second chance to pursue a life filled with passion, adventure and the vast unknown together.

Early Thanksgiving morning Rita and I carried my wedding gown and bridal accessories aboard the aircraft carrier. Bud and David helped us carry everything we would need for the wedding ceremony to the Executive Officer's stateroom. Barney Kelly had insisted Rita and I use his cabin to dress for the wedding. After we were settled, two airmen knocked on the door and handed me a white bed sheet. I was to wrap the sheet around the hem of my wedding gown after we finished dressing. The airmen explained that although they worked hard to keep the aircraft carrier clean they didn't want to risk anything getting on my wedding gown. The airmen had volunteered earlier to escort Rita and me to the fo'c'sle of the ship where the wedding would be held. The rare and unusual procession walked through the hanger bay and passed through the enlisted men's quarters on the way to the fo'c'sle. Many of the sailors had to think they were dreaming as Rita and I passed through their quarters.

Captain Smith had arranged for a curtain to be hung outside a small alcove in the fo'c'sle to allow Rita and me privacy while waiting for the ceremony to begin. The Captain was also there to offer support and calm the jitters of the wedding party. At the appointed time Captain Smith took my arm and proudly walked me down the aisle. I advanced serene, confident and happy.

I looked toward Fran and all my confusion and the emotional dark hole I had been standing at the edge of while making a decision was suddenly gone. All of my doubts disappeared, vaporized into thin air as Fran stood by my side. I wanted this woman, only this woman, to be my partner for the remainder of my days.

A reception at the Officers' Club in Subic Bay followed the wedding ceremony. We warmly greeted everyone who attended. I had even invited the hostesses who worked at the Cubi Officers' Club to come to the wedding reception. Their attendance raised a few eyebrows, but it was such a happy occasion that no one was critical of my actions. Most of the men who knew the hostesses found it humorous.

Later in the afternoon a small ferry took the wedding party and most of the attendees over to Grandee Island to continue the rare Thanksgiving wedding celebration and the fifteenth anniversary of the USS *Enterprise*.

A country western band played and Captain Smith sang a Johnny Cash song while guests laughed and danced in the moonlight. I had reserved one of the cottages on the island for the night. When we retired for the evening Fran lay down on the bed with her head upon the pillow, the windows were open, a cool evening breeze was in the air and I had a woman willing and ready to travel with me one hundred and fifty miles an hour in under three seconds into the future.

A month after the wedding and fairy tale honeymoon in the Philippines, Hong Kong and Singapore, Fran returned to Lemoore. She flew home with the airwing wives and girlfriends who had followed the *Enterprise* as it went from port to port. She re-established her routine of being mother, maintaining the home and participating in the wives squadron functions. Fran and I wrote regularly to one another, and with each letter we were brought one day closer to being together again.

20

Night in the Box

Upon arriving home from our honeymoon my first letter to Bud was to relay how proud I was of Sherri and Sue during my absence. I had hired a young woman to stay with them for the month that I was gone. Because the house payment and utilities would need to be paid and groceries bought while I was away I put Sherri on my checking account. She had just turned sixteen. I took her to the bank and introduced her to the bank manager. I said, "Sherri will be helping me while I am away and will call you if she needs assistance."

She did a superb job. When I returned her little sister, Sue, who was thirteen, said, "Thank God you are home. Sherri was like Scrooge with the money."

Children are amazing how they will step up to the responsibility that is given to them when they know they have your trust. On my first visit to the bank after returning from our honeymoon the bank manager stopped me and said, "I know you are very proud of your daughter. I would like to think my child could do as well."

The saddest day of my honeymoon was Christmas Eve and Christmas morning. Even though my daughters were with their grandparents, surrounded by love and being spoiled, I missed them very much. Bud held me gently in his arms as my tears fell. I had never been away from my daughters over this special holiday. For many years we were like the Three Musketeers with a tradition of making personal gifts and delivering them on Christmas Eve to special friends. Through my tears Bud acknowledged his understanding and sympathy for my pain. He missed his son and we talked about how wonderful our first Christmas would be as a family.

Prior to the regular use of email, international cell phones and texting, letter writing was the primary means of communication with each other when Bud was on cruise or a detachment. Telephone calls only occurred from ports of call so they were rare and expensive. Fortunately as newlyweds we had determined early during our courtship that Bud liked telling stories and I enjoyed reading or hearing about his adventures. I discovered that the longest day, the worst day, the loneliest day could in a heartbeat become the happiest day whenever our mailman delivered a letter from Bud.

Near the end of his cruise with the VA-97 Warhawks the airwing experienced an unusual and traumatic event. After the incident and air operations were secured for the night the flight deck returned to normal. Bud left Air Operations and went down to his stateroom to be alone and write me a letter that told a riveting story.

Night flight operations started out as they had on many other moonless dark evenings. The weather was calm and the deck was pitching slightly as the *USS Enterprise* cruised in the Indian Ocean with Carrier Airwing Nine aboard. Preparations were underway to recover returning aircraft aboard the aircraft carrier. Post–Vietnam War, a typical Western Pacific cruise was one where the aircraft carrier exited the Pacific Ocean and spent several months on station in the Indian Ocean. Strategically the aircraft carrier provided the United States a presence within easy striking distance of the Middle East should Iran initiate aggressive activity resulting in U.S. military action.

One of the major challenges of Indian Ocean operations was the United States did not have strategic allies in the area where the airwing could divert aircraft to land as an alternative to landing aboard the aircraft carrier. Carrier operations outside of the range of friendly airfields were called *Blue Water Operations*. The phrase was coined during flight operations whenever an aircraft carrier transited from the West coast into the Western Pacific. The airwing would fly aircraft between the California coastline and Hawaii with virtually no land in reach for an emergency divert to land an aircraft after launching off the aircraft carrier. Once an aircraft was airborne the options were few, either land back aboard the aircraft carrier, fly into the barricade (which was like a large tennis net that trapped and stopped the aircraft) or eject into the ocean and pray to be rescued safely.

I was a Lieutenant Commander and the operations officer during my department head tour with the VA-97 Warhawks. Because of the inherent risk associated with *Blue Water Operations* at night and aircraft being committed to return to the aircraft carrier, the landing evolutions were typically smaller than normal operations. Two aircraft per squadron would be launched for a total of twelve to fourteen aircraft at one time to recover back aboard the *Enterprise* during most cycles.

The F-14 Tomcats would recover first aboard the carrier because of their high fuel consumption, followed by the A-7B Corsair II, the EA-6B Prowler, and then the E-2 Hawkeye. The KA-6 Tanker and A-6E Intruder served as airborne tankers and would land last. An A-7E Corsair II was regularly configured as a tanker, which was the case for the upcoming night recovery.

In the room adjacent to Air Operations is Carrier Air Traffic Control where airmen monitored all airborne aircraft from departure to landing. Aircraft approaching within fifty miles from the aircraft carrier were assigned a *marshal point* defined by an altitude and distance from the aircraft carrier. Each pilot was given an expected approach time to commence his approach from the *marshal point*. For example, the Marshall Controller would say, "Battlecry 306, hold on the one-hundred-and-fifty-degree radial at angels eleven, twenty-six miles, you're expected approach time is twenty-eight." This meant aircraft 306 would enter a holding pattern at eleven thousand feet on a bearing one hundred and fifty degrees and twenty-eight miles from the aircraft carrier.

The pilot would commence his final approach to the ship from the holding pattern at twenty-eight minutes past the hour. The procedure provided aircraft in holding one thousand feet of clearance and one mile separation from each other as they approached the carrier at one-minute intervals. To ensure everyone was in sync for the exact time the Marshall Controller would give *time hacks* periodically. He would say, "In forty-five seconds the time will be eighteen minutes, five seconds, standby, mark, time is eighteen minutes."

When air operations went perfectly, an aircraft would land every minute. To accommodate the potential for *bolters* (missing all of the wires) or an aircraft being waved off, *bolter holes* were built into the plan to skip a one-minute interval. The one-minute interval would leave a place among the approaching aircraft where Carrier Air Traffic Control would pick up an aircraft that had *boltered*, then gone around and vectored the aircraft back into the landing pattern.

Tom Gravely, an experienced pilot in my sister squadron VA-27 Maces, was on approach in Mace-403. In Air Operations Tom's A-7B Corsair II showed up on the pilot landing aid television (PLAT) in the middle of the crosshairs, putting him right on the glide path. At three-quarter of a mile he was picked up by the landing signal officer (LSO) where radar control said, "Mace-403 you are at three-quarter mile, call the ball." This meant radar control had the aircraft in sight.

Hearing the call was the queue for the pilot to look out of the cockpit he had been flying on instruments and for the first time on the dark night focus on the aircraft carrier. His aircraft was inside a three-quarter mile, and four hundred and fifty feet above the ocean. He could see the outline of the aircraft carrier, the white strobing centerline, the red drop line that would assist in ensuring he was lined up on centerline. The ever important yellow *meatball* on the Fresnel lens illuminated the three-quarter-degree glide slope and was centered between the rows of green datum lights on each side.

As everyone in Air Operations watched, the pilot continued his approach. He seemed to effortlessly keep the aircraft centered on the crosshairs on the PLAT all the way to touchdown. Tom landed and went to full power as expected, but to everyone's surprise the aircraft continued to accelerate down the deck, skipping all of the arresting gear wires. The LSO called, "Bolter, Bolter," on the radio and the PLAT followed Tom's unexpected take off. Once airborne he was picked up immediately by one of the Carrier Air Traffic Control radar controllers and vectored back into one of the built in *bolter holes*. The *bolter holes* were space reserved for an aircraft that had missed all four wires.

Tom was in the landing pattern at twelve hundred feet and vectored back towards the ship. He was passed over to the radar controller for the three-quarter mile ball call and the LSO said, "Roger ball, you're looking good." Again, Tom looked lined up properly on the PLAT, and was right on glide path all the way to touch down. It was another good landing. However, as Tom went to full power, the LSO once more called, "Bolter! Bolter!" He accelerated off the angle deck and back into the black night and where he was again picked up by radar control.

After the second bolter everyone in Air Operations was alert and sitting on the edge of their seats as Mace-403 came back around. Tom landed, only to *bolter* and found himself careening off the angle deck again. The Commanding Officer of VA-27 was summoned to Air Operations and arrived with his maintenance officer. The Commanding Officer and maintenance officer watched Tom make a fourth bolter. The level of anxiety in Air Operations and on the LSO platform, to say nothing of Tom Gravely in the cockpit of Mace-403, had escalated.

Mace-403 was taken out of the holding pattern and vectored to join up with the tanker overhead the ship. He was instructed to take on three thousand pounds of fuel to bring his aircraft back to the maximum gross weight for landing aboard the carrier and to also ensure he could optimize his flight time.

Everyone in Air Operations heard Tom's voice on the radio as Air Operations monitored his tanking evolution. He was clearly shaken from the stress of four night approaches to the carrier and four *bolters*. His voice showed obvious strain as he communicated with the pilot in the A7-B tanker.

I was reminded of a saying made by a World War II carrier pilot who said, "You crash land on the flight deck and hope to catch a wire." During the Vietnam War a physiology study was done on carrier pilots. The study measured their pulse rate, heartbeat, adrenaline and their breathing patterns during actual combat operations and also returning to land back aboard the aircraft carrier. The results showed that pilots were under more severe stress during a night carrier landing than when flying through heavy ground-to-air fire in combat operations. Aviators often described every aircraft carrier landing as a controlled crash. When you added the darkness of night, a pitching flight deck and limited depth perception to the landing approach the level of tension was much higher.

Back aboard the *Enterprise* the landing signal officers reviewed Tom's landing evolution and could not pinpoint that he was doing anything wrong to cause the recurring *bolters*. Tom was getting good carrier controlled approaches and had a nice glide path and power control. He was not dropping the nose at the ramp to catch a wire as less experienced had a tendency to do. Dropping the nose of the aircraft at the ramp was a temptation for some pilots but usually caused a *hook skip bolter*. The VA-27 Commanding Officer and his maintenance officer had the maintenance records of the aircraft in Air Operations and were discussing the history of the aircraft and what might be contributing to the *bolters*. They could find none. The decision was made to put Tom back into the pattern and closely monitor his tailhook upon final touchdown.

For the fifth time Mace-403 was at three-quarter mile, four hundred and fifty feet and calling the ball, but this time in a noticeably high-pitched and shaky voice. By now, pilots in every ready room aboard the aircraft carrier were riveted to their pilot landing aid television and knew exactly what was going through Tom's mind. Air Operations and Tom knew that after a couple more attempts to land aboard the carrier he would be committed to eject from his aircraft into the Indian Ocean at night and rely not only on a safe ejection but a successful helicopter rescue, to say nothing about the loss of a multimillion-dollar aircraft.

Again, Tom crossed the ramp right on glide path and was soaking wet in the cockpit of his aircraft, sweating from anxiety and fear. He felt the crash of the landing gear on the steel flight deck and slammed to full power and prayed he would feel the tug of the arresting gear wire. No such luck. Instead he accelerated off the angle deck, rotated the nose and flew back into the inky black night to be picked up by the radar controller.

The only aircraft left to land aboard were Tom and the A7-B tanker. The Commanding Officer got on the radio with Tom to see how he was doing. The speakers in Air Operations were crystal clear with everyone totally silent as Tom tried to assure his Skipper he was okay. The tone of his voice did not sound at all like Tom. His voice was high pitched and stammering. The Skipper said, "Okay Tom, let's give it one more try and we will talk again if you don't get aboard."

Tom simply said, "Roger."

Paddles called in from the LSO platform and talked to the Air Operations Officer on the phone. He said, "On close observation of the tailhook after the aircraft landed and *boltered* the hook definitely bounced after hitting the flight

Night in the Box

deck. The tailhook moving side to side and bouncing indicated the *snubber pressure* was low." *Snubber pressure* was a nitrogen storage tank below the tailpipe of the aircraft which holds two thousand pounds of pressure on the tailhook. The pressure holds the tailhook in the down position to preclude the hook from bouncing when the aircraft slams into the steel deck at six hundred feet per minute. The *snubber pressure* should hold the hook all the way down as the tailhook engages one of the four arresting gear wires. If Paddles had found the problem and the *snubber pressure* was low it was causing a *soft hook*. Unfortunately, there was no way to pump the *snubber pressure* up while the aircraft was airborne.

By now Mace-403 was back on final approach and called the ball, "Mace-403 ball, three point six fuel."

Paddles said, "Roger ball 403, you're looking real good, just keep it coming." Another nice smooth approach, another excellent landing with the hook moving around like a noodle as the aircraft again careened down the angle deck.

"Mace-403 airborne, this is getting old," Gravely said, as he horsed his Corsair II back into the landing pattern.

Back aboard the ship the Air Boss, Air Operations Officer and the Captain of the *Enterprise* decided on one last-ditch maneuver. As a means of enhancing the probability of the Corsair's tailhook to engage a wire, a yellow shirt stuffed large rolls of toilet paper under the number three wire to prop it up. Air Operations radioed Tom in Mace-403 what the strategy was and for him to fly a slightly slow approach on a short final that would make him cross the ramp a little nose high. The A-7's nose high attitude would cause the tailhook to hang lower below the aircraft. The maneuver was fairly challenging and would only be used in extremis and Tom knew this. His call was, "Mace-403 ball."

From the LSO, "Roger, ball, you're looking good."

Tom expertly crossed the ramp. The tailhook grabbed the three wire and slammed the aircraft to a violent stop. Cheers, clapping and hugs were rampant in Air Operations and the nine ready rooms throughout the aircraft carrier.

I met Tom and his wife at a couple of social functions on the base but did not get to know either one of them well. The first time we met was at an airwing party at the home of the Commanding Officer of the Warhawks. I was sitting on the floor beside Bud talking to one of the squadron wives. Tom came up to Bud and said, "I hear you are marrying some rich bitch from Virginia Beach."

"Tom, I sure am. How would you like to meet her?" Bud asked and winked at me. Bud wrote in a letter after the traumatic evening, "Tom was never quite the same after his '*night in the box*.'"

The airwing returned home from cruise and within six months of the aircraft incident, Tom's full head of brown hair was white as snow. He received orders to shore duty at Naval Air Station Cubi Point in the Philippines. Within the first year of his tour, alone in his room at the Bachelors Officer Quarters, he suffered a massive heart attack and died.

The human body can take only so much!

21

The Art of Partnership

As newlyweds adjustments were necessary and made as we settled into a routine as a military family. Bud and I began our journey filled with passion where everything was new and exciting. When passion, independence and high energy collided it was predictable that misunderstandings and frustrations would erupt. Adapting to the changes within our relationship was an ongoing challenge to two very strong personalities. Like most newlyweds we experienced the occasional fight and flight as we attempted to bring harmony into such opposite temperaments.

I was opinionated and had the ability to push Bud's boundaries and he would become frustrated or angry. I was always willing to defend and ready to fight for my differing position. Our relationship was contrary to Bud's first marriage, and he was not sure what to do. Whether he was out of sorts or distracted he wanted me to read his mind and make the lack of harmony go away. Most of the time he was fortunate and a simple wink, soft smile or appreciative look would dissolve my conflict and whatever had been troubling me would magically disappear. The fight was over before it began, and he was holding out his arms to me and everything would be right with the world. Other times I wanted more than his charismatic smile and the comfort of his arms. He realized I loved his embrace, although it didn't work each and every time. Out of one particular roadside incident there came tremendous growth and a new level of commitment to honor and protect one another.

After Bud completed his department head tour with the VA-97 Warhawks, he was assigned as Flag Secretary to the Admiral of Light Attack Wing Pacific before screening for command. In 1978 he was selected for command and assigned to the VA-146 Blue Diamonds. He would go on cruise as the Executive Officer where the airwing had the honor and privilege of welcoming President Ronald Reagan aboard the *USS Constellation*. Bud had a choice of participating in the airwing flight demonstration performed during the Presidential visit or being in the receiving line to meet the president. He chose to fly and one of his favorite junior officers, Lieutenant George Dom, met the President. The photograph of the President greeting several pilots in the airwing, including George, was on the cover of *Time* magazine. It was an extremely proud day for the Blue Diamonds.

The wives kept busy during the long separation with various fund-raisers and family activities. One fund-raiser escaped a near tragedy following a yard sale at our home. While the wives were finishing up I went inside the house to prepare refreshments. I called out, "My goodness, one of the children must have put a doll in the swimming pool." Immediately I screamed, "Oh no! It's a child," and ran outside and dove into the cold water. I lifted the small child who was floating face down out of the water and into the arms of Liz Leppert. Liz was one of the wives who had been helping with the yard sale and fortunately was a registered nurse. She began CPR while an ambulance was called. The child was three-year-old Erin, the daughter of Carol and Denny Irelan. The ambulance arrived and Erin was rushed to the Naval Air Station Hospital eleven miles away for observation. She was later transported to Valley Children's Hospital in Fresno thirty miles away for additional tests and follow-up. The experience was terrifying for everyone as we waited to hear her prognosis. We arranged for child care for Carol's two older daughters. I notified the Commanding Officer of the Naval Air Station, Captain Mac Gleim, of our situation. He made the proper notification to Bud on the aircraft carrier who would tell Denny of the accident.

We had a squadron phone tree so all the wives who were not at our home were immediately informed of what had happened. I will always believe that the prayers that went out from not only our squadron wives but also from the community were heard and answered. Erin recovered with no physical damage.

My letters to Bud about the near disaster would not arrive for several weeks. In writing I was able to share several personal stories of the kind responses extended to Carol's family by wives and neighbors. Bud would share them with his men. A unique bond was formed within the squadron that time and separation would not break.

After returning home from a six-month Westpac cruise there was a change of command and Bud took over as the Commanding Officer of the Blue Diamonds. During workups and in preparation for the next cruise the squadron deployed temporarily on several detachments. Usually the whole squadron or at least the majority of the squadron would detach for a week or two. They would return home for a short period of time and then leave again for another week or two.

Just as when the squadron returned from cruise there were celebrations, the detachments returning home were also happy occasions. Wives and children were jubilant and excited about the prospect of having Dad home again. Wives were eager for the return of shared responsibilities, nights of laughter, love and lots of sweet pillow talk. Everyone in the family competed for attention.

The defining fight Bud and I experienced was after a detachment returned after being away for a couple of weeks. Bud called me to say the squadron had arrived at the Naval Air Station and invited me to meet him at the Officer's Club for dinner. Several other couples from the squadron would join us. I was excited and happy to see him as the two weeks had been full of challenges for me to handle alone. The car battery had died the morning I was trying to get the girls off to summer camp. I was thankful one of the neighbors delivered the girls to the home of the camp counselor for the trip to the mountains while I waited for AAA to arrive with a new battery.

Frustrations were forgotten. My love was home again and I was excited as always to see him and said, "Of course, what time shall I be there?"

He said, "Come as soon as you can," and hung up the phone.

When I walked into the Officer's Club bar Bud looked over from where he was standing. It was as if he sensed my presence in the way he turned and smiled. His dazzling and charismatic smile was the one that said, "You look stunning as always." The wink I recognized let me know, yep, he had just received the now familiar jolt to his loins.

My heart skipped a beat as I felt his love and appreciation. It was obvious to him that I had taken time to wear something special before coming to the Club. Bud pulled me into the warmth of his arms, held me close savoring my familiar scent and whispered he loved me.

Looking around the Officer's Club we noticed that many of the other wives and children from the squadron had arrived. It was a joyful occasion as families were reunited with one another. The detachment had gone well and everyone was festive. Wives chatted together and men had hands in the air reliving some of the more stimulating events of the past couple of weeks.

In the first year of marriage Bud and I had developed a signal for when we were ready to leave a social event. In fact, it was over an hour since my first signal that I was ready to leave. I was sure he had recognized the signal I had given, but he didn't respond. This was not the first time he chose to ignore my silent message and I had previously explained that as much as I enjoyed the squadron functions I wanted more time alone with him.

My Censor spoke up for the first time in months, "If you love her do not waste one precious minute of your time together." In an attempt to get my Censor to shut up I said, "My time is always being divided between the squadron, home and Fran. Right now the squadron is my main focus. Fran told me the girls are away at camp so we will have the whole weekend to ourselves, except for the squadron cookout tomorrow." I muttered to my Censor, "Go away."

Bud was having fun and looked around the room to find me. He must have noticed that only the bachelors in the squadron remained in the bar when I pulled him aside and pleaded, "Bud, can we please go now? I don't want to drive home alone. We can leave my car on the base and pick it up tomorrow."

"Why don't you go on since you have your car? I will be right behind you."

"Fine, just fine, I am so out of here," I hissed. At least I was sure Bud would say that it had sounded like a hiss to him.

My feelings were already hurt by his delay in leaving the Officer's Club as he attempted to reach out and stop me from leaving, but to no avail. Once I got into my car and had driven through the base security gate I speeded toward home. Bud knew I was very upset and to his credit followed right behind me—with a police car in pursuit.

The police car went ahead of me and forced both of us to pull off to the shoulder of the road. Bud pulled in behind my car and skidded to a stop in the dust and gravel. The officer gave up trying to get me to roll down my window when he saw tears rolling down my cheeks. He turned toward Bud, looking for him to solve this dilemma.

I could hear Bud talking to the police officer in his most persuasive and diplomatic way, saying, "She is royally pissed at me. She asked me to drive her home and I wanted to tell one more flying story. My wife is so stubborn that she will sit there all night before rolling her fucking window down. Frankly I deserve this for being an asshole. I swear, officer, I know better, I just can't seem to help myself until I realize I have hurt her feelings. By the time her feelings are hurt it's too late and I don't know exactly what to do. I just sort of feel my way out of the mess I created and wait for her to respond."

"Have you ever been that way with your wife?" I heard Bud ask the officer.

The police officer hesitated and then with a sympathetic nod over Bud's plight said, "Hell, I live with a woman as stubborn as yours. I have been where you are, but I need the two of you off my highway before someone gets more than their feelings hurt. Do you think you can get her to open the car door and drive her home?"

"Yes, sir," was the quick reply.

Bud walked over to my car with his head down and a look of desperation in his eyes. I opened the car door and he pulled me gently into his arms and reassured me he was totally at fault. Raining soft kisses down my neck he said, "I am so sorry to have been so insensitive to your feelings." His gentle persuasion convinced me he really didn't want me to drive home alone. We left my car on the side of the road and Bud drove carefully the rest of the way home.

I told him I felt foolish for pouting or sulking but sometimes he was so much the *Navy pilot* he seemed to forget about his wife who loved him so much. The fight became unimportant as the acceptance of our differences and interdependence upon one another became the primary focus of our marriage. We learned to balance the Navy lifestyle and the needs of one another. Through trial and error we emerged as a strong couple with a happy marriage by learning to understand and compromise individually and together.

The next morning as we were enjoying breakfast I asked, "What flying adventure was so important that you didn't want to leave the Club last night?"

I said, "A couple of the junior officers wanted me to tell them about the time I was the *tower flower* and Skipper Switzer ejected. I feel I haven't fully explained to you that sometimes happy hour and getting together with the junior officers serves a dual purpose. We play silly games like dead bug and drink a little beer, but it's also a great time for them to ask questions that perhaps they don't want to ask while on duty or questions they wouldn't ask senior officers in their own squadron. Junior officers avidly listen and want to absorb flying stories of those who have served in combat and are more senior to themselves."

"You know me Fran, I love telling stories and didn't want to pass up the opportunity. I wrote you the story on my last cruise aboard the *Constellation*. It was about Bill Switzer's ejection from an F-14 Tomcat."

22
Tower Flower

I WATCHED MY GOOD FRIEND FROM flight school and fellow Commanding Officer of the VF-24 Renegades, Commander Bill Switzer, wheeling his Tomcat into the groove. All looked good as Bill centered up on the crosshairs of the pilot landing aid television (PLAT) that recorded every landing and take-off from the aircraft carrier. The flight deck was clear, and we anticipated a normal landing as the big bird swooped in. The wheels smoked as they hit the steel deck just in front of the number three target wire. The Tomcat squatted as the nose wheel hit the deck. The tailhook skipped the number three wire and grabbed the number four wire as Bill slammed the power on the big F-14 jet engines all the way forward. In most landings the arresting gear wire brought the aircraft to a rapid but controlled stop.

I was in the tower during a typical day of flight operations aboard the *USS Constellation*. The *Connie* was underway in the Indian Ocean with Carrier Air Group Nine aboard. I was the Commanding Officer of the VA-146 Blue Diamonds on a six-month deployment. Throughout day flight operations each squadron was required to have a pilot in Pri-Fly, or the tower.

I was assigned the watch in the tower, colloquially referred to as the *tower flower*, for the 1530 recovery. From Pri-Fly, I could see the landing area, which included the LSO platform and all four arresting gear wires. I could also see the bow of the aircraft carrier where the four catapults are located. The *tower flower* was stationed in Pri-Fly to answer questions from the Air Boss if a potential problem should arise from one of the squadron pilots. Another reason for having a squadron pilot in the tower was to observe and ensure proper procedures were followed by pilots when they taxied aircraft on the flight deck. The *tower flower* watched every catapult shot, clearing turn, entry into the break and landing. He observed whether or not each pilot maintained the correct interval between landing aircraft back aboard the carrier. He also kept a log on each flight evolution and debriefed a pilot who did not conform to proper procedures after flight operations were completed.

Flight operations aboard every aircraft carrier flight deck are designed with multiple redundancies imbedded in each critical evolution of take-off and landing. During the 1980s there were five different types of fixed wing aircraft in the airwing aboard the *Connie* as well as several types of rotary wing or helicopter aircraft. Fixed wing aircraft included the A-7 Corsair II, F-14 Tomcat, A-6 Intruder, KA-6 Intruder tanker, S-3 Viking and the turbo-prop E-2 Hawkeye. Each type of aircraft had its own approach speed for landing back aboard the aircraft carrier.

The *USS Constellation* had four arresting gear wires, each of which were attached to the large arresting gear engines located below the flight deck landing area. The arresting gear engines were simply very large hydraulic engines which were designed to pay out the arresting gear wire after the tailhook engaged one of them. As they pay out aircraft are brought to a violent but safe stop. A function called constant speed run-out kept the aircraft on or near the centerline when landing. The maximum landing weight of each aircraft was determined by the empty gross weight of the aircraft plus fuel and external stores. The arresting gear wires were manually set to the maximum gross weight for the type aircraft in line to land next aboard the carrier. As an example, the F-14 Tomcat's gear was set for sixty thousand pounds.

The Air Boss was in charge of all flight operations that took place on the flight deck. From Pri-Fly he and the Assistant Air Boss monitored the settings for the gross weight of all catapult shots and landings. In the case of landings, the arresting gear engine was actually set in the arresting gear room by a junior enlisted man. The Assistant Air Boss in Pri-Fly selected the type of aircraft on a repeater that showed up on the bow catapult walks and in the arresting gear room.

The electronic repeater on the edge of the flight deck where the arresting gear officer monitored recoveries would display the same weight, sixty thousand pounds. The airman assigned to talk in Pri-Fly also passed the type aircraft and gross weight over the sound powered radio phone to each arresting gear room. The airman in the arresting gear room actually set the gear at sixty thousand pounds and announced on the sound powered phones, "gear set, F-14, sixty thousand pounds." This process was repeated in each of the four arresting gear rooms to reset each of the wires at the appropriate setting each and every time an aircraft landed.

As the *tower flower* for my A-7 Corsair squadron, I watched flight deck operations as my squadron's four aircraft launched successfully off the bow of the ship. After all aircraft were launched catapult operations were secured and everyone in the tower shifted their eyes to the stern of the carrier where landing operations had begun. Normally the recovery goes very smoothly. When an aircraft's wheels hit the flight deck the pilot ALWAYS goes to full power immediately. If the aircraft missed all four wires the jet engines were running at full power and could propel the aircraft airborne again. If an aircraft landing missed all four wires it was called a *bolter*. Day *bolters* were not common and relatively benign; however, at night *bolters* were much more dangerous and challenging.

The F-14 Tomcats were first to land because of their high fuel consumption. I watched as four Tomcats swept over the ship in tight echelon formation at eight hundred feet and after crossing the bow initiated a *carrier break* with their hooks down. The break was done by the first aircraft rapidly rolling into a sixty- to seventy-degree bank and pulling the stick back abruptly to make a sharp left hand one-hundred-and-eighty-degree turn downwind paralleling the ships course but in the opposite direction.

The other three pilots executed the same break at three-second intervals, pulling four-plus g's. The pilot would keep the nose of the Tomcat on the horizon in a level break until steady downwind. He then eased the g's and allowed the big F-14 to slow down to one hundred and eighty knots or two hundred and eight miles per hour while descending to six hundred feet and lowered the landing gear and flaps. Pulling back on the power, the pilot trimmed the nose of the aircraft up as it continued to decelerate to the optimum angle of attack, which was the most desirable landing speed for a given aircraft at its present gross weight.

Approaching abeam of the LSO platform, slightly forward of the stern on the port side, the pilot initiated a gentle forty-five-degree left turn. He maintained his airspeed by holding the optimum angle of attack, easing the stick forward to descend to the ninety-degree position at four hundred and fifty feet. At this point the pilot anticipated seeing the *meatball* on the Fresnel lens, which was the landing aid system that indicated to the pilot he was on or off the prescribed three-and-one-half-degree glide slope. When the pilot looked out to his port side of the canopy, just after crossing over the wake of the aircraft carrier, and saw the yellow *meatball light* he knew if he was high or low based on the position of the *meatball* relative to the green datum lights on either side of the ball. The pilot pressed the radio transmit button with his thumb on the inside of the throttles and called, "201 Tomcat ball, state four point five." This meant that he was piloting an F-14 Tomcat, side number 201 and had the *meatball* visually and the aircraft fuel state was four thousand five hundred pounds.

The landing signal officer was the only one on the frequency who responded with, "Roger ball." This was a very important call, particularly to the men down in the arresting gear room. They can't hear the pilot's call so it was relayed to them by the sound powered phone from Pri-Fly. This no doubt oversimplifies the process that was repeated every time an aircraft landed, and most of the time safely, but NOT ALWAYS.

The *tower flower* and everyone else in Pri-Fly knew the identity of the pilot of each aircraft because it was written on a big Plexiglas grease pencil board in Pri-Fly with the side number of the aircraft and name of the pilot. This was important, especially at night, in order for the air operations representative to know the relative proficiency level of a pilot should he get into trouble and need additional assistance when landing back aboard the carrier.

From inside the tower I observed a violent deceleration as the hydraulic power of the arresting gear engines decelerated the big jet from one hundred and thirty miles per hour to zero in less than six hundred feet. The pilot was slammed forward in his harness, head jolting forward and down under the deceleration, after which normally the aircraft would be stopped on the flight deck at full power. After landing the pilot would pull the power to idle and raise the arresting hook to spit out the wire. The pilot's attention would then go quickly to the yellow shirt on the flight deck who would signal him to immediately raise the hook, power up and taxi clear of the landing area so that the aircraft behind him could land safely in less than forty-five seconds.

Not this time. As Skipper Switzer advanced the power to full, the jet leaped forward and continued to accelerate as the arresting gear wire streamed out like spaghetti. The wire continued to race out of its protective tracks, and then, BOOM. The Tomcat reached the end of the arresting gear wire that had been tightly reeled in the large containment area in the arresting gear room. The aircraft shuddered as it quickly slowed from the explosion of the number four arresting gear engine in the catapult room. Then, the Tomcat began slowly picking up speed, but certainly not enough to fly.

The flames of the afterburners lit when Skipper Switzer selected afterburner in a futile effort to achieve flying speed. When the aircraft ambled off the angle deck and started to descend toward the sea with the nose rising, Skipper Switzer attempted to get the big jet to climb, but to no avail. The Tomcat continued to descend and then started a slow roll to port, below the flight deck.

I watched the smoke of the canopy jettisoning, followed very closely by the back seat firing Lieutenant Dave (Bio) Baranek, the Radar Intercept Officer, out of his cockpit, and right behind him Skipper Switzer's seat fired. The aircraft continued a slow roll almost ninety degrees to port by the time Skipper Switzer's seat actually left the aircraft. He shot straight out of the aircraft at a ninety-degree angle. Bio's parachute had opened when he was about one hundred feet over the water and the parachute made a half of a swing before being slammed into the sea. Commander Switzer was not so lucky. He was ejected straight out parallel to the ocean and slammed into the sea still in his ejection seat. I was sure he would not survive.

Fran quickly picked up on my emotions and shock and interjected, "How horrible to watch yet another good friend crash into the sea."

"Yes, it was difficult to watch and be unable to stop what was happening. The good news was that there was always a rescue helicopter (RESCAP) flying off the starboard stern of the aircraft carrier during day and night flight operations. These highly skilled pilots and rescue crews spent hours of boredom in what was called starboard delta, or circling abeam the stern in a starboard circle. They are the airwing private angels on alert in the event of a crash or ejection."

The helicopter was over the crash site in minutes. A sling with a rescue crewman lowered over the downed Radio Intercept Officer who was tangled in his parachute lines and in danger of drowning. The downwash of the rotor blades increased the closer the helicopter got to the water and made it difficult for the RESCAP crewman to see. He was able to attach the pelican hook to Bio's torso harness and free him from his tangled parachute lines. He signaled for his squadron mates in the helicopter to lift Bio and him to safety. Once they were safe the helicopter quickly transitioned overhead, and Skipper Switzer amazingly appeared upright in the water, arms in the air signaling he was waiting to be picked up.

Next, the RESCAP crewman expertly prepared Skipper Switzer for extraction by placing him in a sling after ascertaining that he was not severely injured. With a wave from the crewman Commander Switzer was lifted out of the water with the eerie sheen of rotor blades surrounding him. The airwing private angels had performed another miracle. The RIO, Lieutenant Dave Baranek, was uninjured; Commander Bill Switzer sustained a minor back injury. Both returned to the flight schedule within a month.

All naval aviation accidents have the laborious task of finding out what went wrong and why. With each accident there are two separate investigations. First, the accident investigation attempts to determine why the accident happened and second, the Judge Advocate General, or JAG, investigation was to determine any legal liabilities that might exist.

Fran asked, "What legal liabilities could be involved?"

"One example that comes to mind was when a retired admiral and former Director of the Central Intelligence Agency assisted a family in a civil law suit against the former Commanding Officer of the *USS Kitty Hawk* after the death of their son aboard the aircraft carrier. The law suit determined his death was caused by a catapult crew error."

I was the senior officer of nine Commanding Officers in Carrier Airwing Nine. Commander Switzer was the second senior officer, and since the reviewing officer must always be senior to the person who had the accident I became the Chairman of the accident investigation. First I looked into the basics of the redundant systems aboard the aircraft carrier. Redundant systems are in place and should preclude an accident from happening. I discovered how even redundant systems can fail. Whenever a human being is in the loop, there is always a risk of error.

With the immensity of operations on an aircraft carrier and all the interlinking systems and personnel that combine to make flight operations at sea possible, an accident investigation was both time and energy consuming. The investigation took five weeks while normal flight operations continued.

After interviewing dozens of ship's personnel, both officers and enlisted men, it was determined several causal factors were clearly apparent. First, the least flagrant cause of the accident was the electronic flight deck repeater was inoperable. The electronic repeater was located on the starboard catwalk near the number four arresting gear wire where the flight deck officer stands during flight operations and signals when the deck is clear. In this case the repeater for the number four wire was not functioning. The investigation revealed that the electronic repeater was inoperable and had been for an extended period of time. The repeater was one of several in the system that showed each of the four arresting gear engines was set at the appropriate weight for approaching aircraft. In this case the F-14 Tomcat was set at sixty thousand pounds. Again, this was not the more serious of the two failures. However, had the electronic repeater been operable and the Flight Deck Officer looked at it he would have known that the number four arresting gear engine was still set at zero and not have given the signal for a clear deck to land.

The second and most egregious error was the following: It was mid-morning on the aircraft carrier and each of the catapult engine rooms had three watch standers during flight operations, a senior Petty Officer and two lower ranking enlisted airmen. The night before the accident one of the two airmen had a watch from midnight to six a.m. and had not been to bed. The engine room needed to be painted, so the senior Petty Officer left the young airman who had been on watch all night the task of resetting the gear while he manned a paint brush and the other airman monitored the actual arresting gear engine.

After each landing or *trap*, the gear was reset to zero until it was known what the next aircraft to land would be. The next aircraft up was an F-14, and this was radioed to each of the engine rooms and flight deck control from Pri-Fly. At this point each of the airmen in charge of setting the gear from zero to sixty thousand pounds responded after manually setting the gear "number one set F-14, sixty thousand pounds, number two set F-14, sixty thousand pounds, number three set F-14, sixty thousand pounds and number four set F-14, sixty thousand pounds."

Not so fast! The number four gear operator who had been up all night on watch said, "Gear set F-14, sixty thousand pounds," and abruptly nodded off to sleep before setting the gear. The gear remained at the zero setting.

Commander Bill Switzer made what would have been a near-perfect day landing by engaging the number four wire after skipping the three wire. He slammed the power to full and braced for a violent arrested landing. Instead, his aircraft leaped forward as the arresting gear wire streamed with minimal resistance until it reached the end of the line. At that point two blocks of balsa wood are smashed together in the arresting gear room in an attempt to reduce damage. At full speed, as happened here, when they are blocked there is an explosion and the arresting gear equipment and hydraulic fluid flow dangerously around the small space. On the rare occasions that this happens, crewmen in the arresting gear room may be killed or injured.

In the end an aircraft was lost, but not a life. The JAG investigation concluded there was no liability to be assigned. The accident investigation found fault with the Air Department, but no one received punitive action. Flying off and landing aboard an aircraft carrier continues to be a dangerous business and shit happens!

23
A Road Well Travelled

As children Bud and I lived in rural America. However, that is where the similarity ended. Bud's childhood was centered around rivers and streams with his family in Oregon until he joined the Navy. On the opposite end of the spectrum was my totally dysfunctional childhood where I was shuffled from family to family, town to town in the rich agricultural San Joaquin Valley of California. Where I continually prayed to find a home where I would be wanted and loved.

Our mutual view of the world would continue to expand dramatically during our tour at the National War College, in Washington, D.C. It was the most prestigious of all military service colleges in the United States. Bud attended the college in 1983 with around one hundred and twenty senior officers from each of the services as well as senior civilians from the CIA, DIA, FBI, State Department and FEMA.

The War College was a welcome reprieve from Bud's previous command responsibilities. While he was the Commanding Officer of the Blue Diamonds his squadron deployed over three hundred days of his eighteen-month tour.

Students were exposed to the process of high-level government strategy and international relationship building. One of the highlights of the year for

Bud was having the time and opportunity to train for and run the Marine Corps Marathon. He considered the year at the National War College his *athletic scholarship,* and running the marathon was one of the proudest accomplishments of his life. He was forty years old and his goal was to run the event in under four hours. On a cold wintery day he crossed the finish line at three hours and fifty-three minutes. Several of Bud's classmates made the journey with him along the twenty-six-mile trek.

After he cooled down under an aluminum cape we went directly to join classmates at the Gangplank Restaurant. He was as high as a kite. I'm sure people in the restaurant thought he was high on something other than life. Bud shared with the group, "Hains Point was the twenty-mile point and when I trained for the marathon it was the most difficult and lonely point in my run." Hains Point is located on the southern tip of East Potomac Park between the main branch of the Potomac River and the Washington Channel in southwest Washington, D.C.

Bud continued, "As I arrived at Hains Point on the day of the marathon a supporter with his dog was playing music on a boom box at full blast. The music was to the theme from the movie, *Rocky.* It was incredible the way the adrenaline pumped throughout my body and the final miles were made easy."

For years afterwards Bud and his dog, believing one good deed desires another, would go to Hains Point during the Marine Marathon and play the music from *Rocky* for the runners. As some of the runners approached it appeared they could barely run or walk, and after hearing the music they would be revitalized and run over and hug him and say thank you before continuing their run.

There were three notable students in the class of 1983. First was Army General Wesley K. Clark, West Point graduate and Rhodes Scholar. General Clark joined the race for the Democratic Party presidential nomination in 2004, but later withdrew and campaigned for Senator John Kerry. Second was General Hugh Shelton, who later served two terms as the Chairman of the Joint Chiefs of Staff under Bill Clinton and George W. Bush. He was the first Green Beret to serve as Chairman. The third notable classmate was Ms. Barbara McNamara, who held the number two position at the National Security Agency and was the first woman to be named Deputy Director for Operations.

A Road Well Travelled

Looking through the archives of notable past students we found former Secretary of State and Chairman of the Joint Chiefs of Staff Colin Powell and Republican Presidential nominee and United States Senator John McCain.

While Bud was training for the Marine Corps Marathon he often jogged on the base at Fort Lesley McNair. Fort McNair is where the National War College and the Industrial College of the Armed Forces are located. The 3rd U.S. Infantry (The Old Guard) also trained and practiced their drills on weekends on the historic base. Early on a Saturday morning as Bud jogged, his run was interrupted by a small caravan of black SUVs moving slowly along the inner perimeter of the base with men in black suits walking alongside the automobiles. The caravan was protecting the President of the United States, George Herbert Walker Bush. Bud stopped his run to watch the President jog past with his entourage following closely behind.

He said, "All of a sudden there was a loud pop of simultaneous gunfire. At lightning speed the secret service agents literally tackled the President and threw him into the back seat of one of the waiting SUVs and the entourage sped quickly away." Thankfully President Bush was not harmed. Bud said, "I was certain that the head of the security detail lost his Presidential security job. Evidently the Secret Service had not coordinated with the Old Guard on the base. A part of the Old Guard training involved firing their muskets, pointed into the air, from a crisp military formation. The musket fire triggered the Secret Service team to react."

The second highlight of the year for Bud was travelling with fellow students from the War College throughout the world and meeting face to face with senior military and civilian officials in other countries. The trip was two weeks of international travel with a distinct and vast disparity between countries. A lottery was held to decide what group of students would go to selected countries.

Bud's group of classmates drew Norway, Denmark and Sweden. During the trip his group was exposed to critical military bases, viewed flight demonstrations, and toured ships, submarines and harbor installations. They also met with senior civilian government leaders. While touring in Denmark the group was surprised to see the Queen Mother walking on the street ahead of them. She turned and smiled as if they were long-time friends before getting into her chauffeur-driven Rolls-Royce.

In Denmark they also saw the famous bronze mermaid. Hans Christian Anderson wrote the *Little Mermaid* fairy tale in 1837, and in 1909 the founder of Carlsberg Breweries (which they toured) was fascinated by the story and had the statue built. The *Little Mermaid* was less than five feet tall, much smaller than any of them expected, and sat on a rock near shore looking out to sea. Bud thought it amazing that a small statue, less than five feet tall, over one hundred years old, was recognized throughout the world.

In Sweden the group flew by helicopter to an outlying airfield where they watched a demonstration of the Swedish Virgin aircraft. One of the interesting stops was a tour in Norway and seeing F-16 Falcons hidden in underground revetments to preclude observation from satellite intelligence of foreign countries.

During the year Bud also joined a group of professional counselors who were working with young felons in Washington that had been convicted of a multitude of major crimes and were undergoing rehabilitation after they were released from the local jails. Bud and his counseling partner centered their therapy on group dynamics. They believed that by working with the group as a team they would produce positive results. Bud and his partner met every two weeks with ten to fifteen of the young men. He said, "Our goal was that given time and opportunity we could aid in repatriating most any person." Well, not so fast.

The counseling dynamics centered on positive thinking as a way to change their lives. The philosophy was similar to the *Laws of Attraction* or "birds of a feather flock together." They attempted to get the young men to understand that they are what they think about and remain like those they associate or surround themselves.

On one occasion they took the group to an air show at Andrews Air Force Base. A Boy Scout troop was visiting at the same time. They were with a dozen black teenagers, most of whom had no male role model, no chance of a college education or the ability to join the military or become a commissioned officer. None of them could conceive of flying a fighter jet. Unless their criminal records were expunged when they turned eighteen they could not join the military as an enlisted person with the opportunity of promotion or going to school. At the air show the group showed little or no interest in the activities whereas the Boy Scouts were crawling all over the aircraft on display. Bud's group gravitated to the fast food booths for cokes and hot dogs. Bud said, "I was shocked at their visible lack of interest or excitement in what has kept me captivated for my whole adult life. This was a complete a surprise to me."

In the six months Bud worked with the group not one of them showed the slightest degree of interest in changing their lives. The *coup de grâce* came as he drove some of them home to their housing areas after counseling in his white Cadillac Seville with chrome wheels. This was a real treat to them. The teenagers would turn up the volume on the radio and talk about what a wonderful *pimp mobile* this would make and what a great business they could do if they had a fancy car to drive.

The year in Washington, D.C., was wonderful as well as educational for Bud and me as we took advantage of living in the nation's capital. We visited the museums, rode our bicycles to national monuments and listened to patriotic open air concerts in the warm summer months. We particularly enjoyed the Army Twilight Tattoo on the Ellipse at the Jefferson Memorial or on the grounds of the Washington Monument. The Tattoo featured the 3rd U.S. Infantry (The Old Guard), the U.S. Army Band and the U.S. Army Drill Team. The patriotic display and majesty of the ceremony was a reminder of the traditions and sacrifices made by men and women in our armed forces.

Wives were invited to attend unclassified lectures at the War College. Ethics and the Vietnam War was a favorite seminar, and I particularly enjoyed the discussions of the students in the class. They discussed how it seemed that whenever atrocities occur somewhere in the world our government we send in troops whether or not our citizens are supportive of the cause.

I wanted to know what it was like to fight in Vietnam and return home to an unappreciative populace after the sacrifices they had made. They said, "When we joined the military we pledged an oath to protect and defend our nation from enemies foreign and domestic." We were just doing our duty.

The Vietnam War had brought unprecedented change within the country. Citizens believed they were being lied to by the government and their frustration and anger led to protests and demonstrations not previously seen on such a national scale. Instead of the class members being offended by the demonstrations they accepted the sacrifices required of war and the burden placed on the few. Demonstrations only served to reinforce the students' belief that they were willing to give their lives to protect the rights and freedom of all Americans. I was fortunate to have the opportunity to sit in class, listen, learn and admire these courageous men and women.

A dramatic event occurred during April of the school year. A bomb was placed in a flowerpot on the front steps of the rotunda in the middle of the night, and it exploded. Windows were blown out and the historic building sustained some structural damage. Above the front atrium of the college was a magnificent bronze statue of a golden eagle which was destroyed in the blast. The unknown group was never found and the phrase "*act of terrorism*" was a new term to be used in our society, a term that soon would become almost commonplace.

After graduation from the War College the next set of orders Bud received was joyful news to both of us. We were extremely pleased that Bud was assigned as the Executive Assistant to Commander Naval Air Force Atlantic (COMNAVAIRLANT). He would be working directly for our good friend, Admiral Carol C. Smith. The assignment to the Admiral's staff meant regular short business trips and occasions for formal receptions and catered dinner parties at the Admiral's quarters on the Norfolk Naval Air Station in Virginia. But more important, there would be time for days on the beach and casual dinner parties at our home on Atlantic Avenue in Virginia Beach. That's right, after seven years, Bud's orders would return me to familiar surroundings for a year and time to be near the water only blocks away from my old home on 72nd Street.

Since our wedding aboard the *USS Enterprise* we had grown very fond of Admiral Smith, not just for his mentoring and generosity during our courtship but also for the friendship which had matured through the years. Bud traveled extensively with Admiral Smith as one of his senior aides. The Naval Base in Cuba was under the Admiral's responsibility and the staff took a trip to the Guantanamo Bay Naval Base, also known as GITMO. GITMO is located on the shores of Guantanamo Bay on the southeastern end of Cuba. Admiral Smith and Bud toured the area and looked out with fascination across the guarded fence into no man's land. Isolation permeated the air, and in 2002 the base became the site of the Guantanamo Detention Center, holding terrorists who continue to threaten the security of our country.

Travelling often with the Admiral made us aware of personal hardships the Admiral was dealing with on a regular basis, in addition to his military responsibilities. More important, the Admiral was experiencing intermittent chest pain and doctors were treating him for an ulcer. Accepting treatment for the ulcer was his way of dealing with what he feared to be causing the pain. The Admiral's father had died of a massive heart attack when he was in his early fifties. He was having symptoms very similar to those his father experienced before his fatal attack.

One weekend as Admiral Smith and I walked quietly on the beach he asked me, "The doctors have not been able to diagnosis my symptoms. Fran, do you think my chest pain could just be in my head?"

Unaware of the seriousness of his question I attempted to reassure him his distress was an indication that something was physically wrong and he should follow up with another opinion.

A week later Admiral Smith and Bud flew to Iceland on a short trip to visit the United States Naval Air Station in Keflavik, an important base under his area of responsibility. A P-3 Orion Anti-Submarine Warfare Airwing was stationed on the naval base. The P-3 community had the enormous responsibility of tracking Soviet submarines in the North Atlantic during the Cold War.

When Admiral Smith and Bud returned from Iceland and landed at the Norfolk Naval Air Station he called and asked me to join the family at the Admiral's quarters for an early dinner. Bud said, "The Admiral wants to go for a run before dinner. Please join us in a couple of hours."

I was ready to leave for Norfolk when Bud called crying, "Franny, he's gone. The Admiral is dead. He died in my arms. We were at the end of our run, and you know I never ran ahead of him. This time I did, and when I looked back I saw him slap his chest. Perspiration spewed off of his body. He stumbled forward and fell with his head striking the asphalt. One of Admiral Wes McDonald's support staff called for an ambulance and helped administer CPR. However, it was too late to resuscitate him." The autopsy report revealed Admiral Smith had died from a massive heart attack and most likely was dead before his head hit the ground.

We were available twenty-four seven to help the Admiral's wife, Sara Jane, and the Navy administer the many details of the funeral and changes within the staff. Sara Jane asked Bud to pick up their youngest daughter from school and tell her the Admiral had died. The incredible man who had walked me down the aisle and gave me away at our wedding would not be there to do the same for his daughter.

This was not the first time Bud had been asked to tell a child that they had lost their father. In fact, I knew exactly how difficult it was because previously a friend and neighbor's husband was killed while on cruise. The wife asked Bud and me to tell her two young sons. Two young boys would shed tears of sorrow and find the strength to comfort their grieving mother.

Bud said, "It is a trust beyond comprehension to be asked by a wife to tell her child of the death of his or her father. By accepting the responsibility you allow the spouse time to grieve privately before responding to her child's grief."

He did it well, and I was very proud of his ability to offer comfort at such a sad time. It was more difficult for me. I felt myself literally absorb the raw inconsolable pain of loss and despair as two young boys sat sobbing as if their hearts would break apart.

In the days ahead our primary role was to assist in carrying out the burden of the reception after the funeral, help with thank-you notes, the transition and moving arrangements. The family would need to move from their quarters within the month. The incoming Admiral and his family were scheduled to move into Admiral Smith's quarters.

Admiral Wes McDonald was a four-star admiral and Commander in Charge of the Atlantic Fleet. He was Admiral Smith's boss, neighbor and good friend. He approached Bud at the funeral reception with condolences. He thanked Bud and me for what we had done in assisting with the events associated with the Navy's tragic loss. Admiral McDonald recognized the depth of our grief and said he was sending us on a Navy aircraft to Bermuda for a week so we could grieve privately.

We had a beautiful suite on Naval Air Station Bermuda with time to explore the island and mourn the loss of our friend. It was a difficult week for both of us as we came to terms with the realization we had each lost someone special. To Bud, the Admiral represented the older brother he never had, and for me, the father figure I always dreamed of having as a child. When we looked back on the week, we talked about how alone we felt and yet we were always together. Our love making brought only temporary relief from the pain. We were both needy and wanted to be consoled and at times lashed out at one another inappropriately. It was not easy but through patience and love we were able to reach a point where we found strength and comfort to deal with the loss both individually and as a couple, and we made peace with our loss.

Years later Bud and I were interested in the 1992 investigative report on television labeling the Bermuda Naval Air Station as the *Club Med* of the Navy. The report cited its use by senior military and U.S. government officials, deeming the base a de facto vacation retreat. When we stayed at the base in Bermuda Bud was not a senior ranking officer, but we appreciated the thoughtfulness of Admiral MacDonald to allow us to travel and stay on the naval air station.

In 1995 the U.S. facilities in Bermuda were closed except for the NASA tracking station on Coopers Island at the eastern end of NAS Bermuda. In actuality the base closure was the result of the military reducing the requirements for the Air Station through the development of sophisticated U.S. military equipment.

24
A Cat and Trap

I CONCLUDED MY TOUR WITH COMNAVAIRLANT and was selected to command the VA-122 Flying Eagles Replacement Air Group. Just as the Replacement Air Group (RAG) was a welcomed bonus command for my previous mentor, Captain John Nicholson, it was the same for me. Fran and I returned to Naval Air Station Lemoore, California. As the Commanding Officer of VA-122 the experience was rewarding by associating with class after class of young excited Naval Aviators. A new class of aviators reported to the squadron every six weeks, eager to fly the Ling Temco Vought A7-E Corsair II. Fran and I made a dedicated effort to get to know each pilot and his family by holding informal dinner parties in our home for the incoming classes. Dinner was always served buffet style with Fran's homemade lasagna; two department head wives, Liz Leppert and Robin Roberson, would prepare and serve dessert. After dinner I would go around the room and ask each of the pilots to share something about his background, in order to become better acquainted. At night as we prepared for bed Fran and I talked about what the future held for these talented young officers and their spouses. History rewarded us with reports of success after success.

I valued the discipline of the training environment and my personal challenge was to ensure these Naval Aviators received the best instruction in the world. I stayed closely involved and flew with each detachment to Fallon, Nevada, for weapons training. I also joined each new class of pilots as they completed day and night carrier qualifications aboard the USS *Lexington* in Pensacola, Florida.

As the Commanding Officer of the Flying Eagles I was fortunate to be able to schedule my eleven-year-old son, Shane, and I time to fly the FA-18 Hornet dome simulator during Shane's summer visit to see us. Simulators were often used to augment additional pilot training. The dome is a three-hundred-and-sixty-degree full-motion simulator where two pilots are in separate cockpit mock-ups. The simulator domes have spheres with a high-quality movie screen on the ceiling and a full three-hundred-and-sixty-degree view right down to a mock-up of the ground below. It is as close to the actual experience as one can imagine, without actually being in the air.

Inside the simulator the pilots are vectored into a *merge* where they meet head on at over five hundred miles per hour and engage in air combat maneuvering. Each aircraft is loaded with simulated Sidewinder and Sparrow missiles and twenty-millimeter machine gun bullets, along with the normal load of fuel for the mission.

I was in one cockpit and Shane in the other. He was being heavily coached by the RAG flight instructors. Shane fired all of his missiles before the merge and in theory would have had none left to fire. His flight instructors continued to reload him with missiles and bullets, and gave him additional fuel so he could defeat his Dad! I had limited ordinance and fuel which was a normal part of the Rough Raiders training syllabus. A pilot learned to *husband his resources* in order to make the kill.

Shane was well coached, had great pilot instruction, unlimited fuel and ordinance and began to actually threaten me. I became more defensive and worked harder to defeat him. When the flight instructors realized the extent of my aggression they came up privately on the intercom and said, "Skipper, do you really want to kill your son?" I had become overly competitive, determined to win and forgot who I was fighting against!

My predecessor, as the Commanding Officer of VA-122 Flying Eagles, set a quota where two or three pilots would be disqualified from each class during night carrier qualification training. Rather than follow that inane process, I put the onus on the landing signal officers to train better and work smarter with student pilots who showed less-natural skills. As a result, every student graduated from VA-122 and went to the fleet while I was in command. Of importance to note, none of them returned from the fleet for poor performance.

Lieutenant Bob Ferry was a unique success story. When I took over as the Commanding Officer of VA-122 Bob had disqualified twice during night carrier landings and was in the squadron as an officer awaiting non-flying orders to the fleet. I worked personally with the LSOs to get Lieutenant Ferry back into the program. He was able to successfully complete day and night carrier qualifications aboard the aircraft carrier.

Later when I was the Operations Officer in Carrier Task Force Seventy in the Philippines I told my boss, Rear Admiral Denny Brooks, Lieutenant Bob Ferry's success story. One afternoon the Admiral and I prepared to fly ashore from the *USS Midway* in the S-3 Viking Carrier Onboard Delivery aircraft (COD). After we climbed into the back and strapped into the aircraft, the pilot in the left seat turned around with a big toothy grin and said, "Welcome aboard, Skipper."

Admiral Brooks said, "That was nice. Who is he?"

I laughed mischievously and replied, "Remember the story I told you about Lieutenant Bob Ferry in VA-122? Well, that's him."

Admiral Brooks squirmed uneasily in his seat and said, "Are you sure we need to go to this meeting?" Bob did a great job in flying his captive brass ashore.

One final note I'll add about my command tour. There were five Class-A accidents (loss of aircraft) during my predecessor's tour as the Commanding Officer of VA-122. By emphasizing safety procedures during my eighteen-month command there were zero. I attributed my personal involvement with my flight instructors, landing signal officers and every young pilot as making the difference.

Saying farewell to the Replacement Air Group and Lemoore, my next orders were eighteen challenging months with Carrier Task Force Seventy (CTF-70) in the Philippines as the Operations Officer. The tour in the Philippines was personally rewarding for Fran and I with the opportunity to make lifetime friends. We shared international events that occurred throughout our months in the Philippines with the staff and their families.

Prior to our arrival and significant was the assassination of the opposition leader Benigno Aquino, who ran against Ferdinand Marcos in 1983. After we arrived in the Philippines Marcos continued his rise to absolute power and corrupt practices within his administration. Muslim guerrilla insurgencies gained strength in Mindanao, further eroding the Ferdinand Marcos presidency and finally leading to his demise.

In the evening hours of February 1986, Marcos and his wife Imelda, with their sixty-member entourage, fled the grounds of the Presidential Palace in Manila to Hawaii and exile. Military families watched their televisions as reporters and film crews recorded small aircraft flying around the palace. After the coup, Lieutenant General Williams, the Commander at Clark Air Force Base who had orchestrated flying President Marcos out of the country, was allegedly poisoned. During these significant historical events an aircraft carrier was held off shore to transport U.S. families to safety had it become necessary.

The Manila International Airport closed several times during the upheaval. A group of wives, including Fran, had gone on holiday to meet husbands on the CTF-70 staff. After they arrived in Pattaya Beach, Thailand, the Manila Airport closed. Arrangements had to be made to fly them back into the Philippines on a C-130 Hercules Navy transport aircraft. The wives rode home in the cargo area, sitting on nylon strap seats like you may have seen in an old John Wayne movie set during World War II. At least that was what it seemed like to Fran. The *coup de grâce* the Navy required the wives to pay for the trip back to their home in the Philippines.

Two exciting trips were offered to the wives of the senior officers of the CTF-70 staff. The first was the opportunity to fly aboard the aircraft carrier *USS Midway* in a C-2A Carrier Onboard Delivery (COD) aircraft. We wore flight suits, headphones and the crew assisted in attaching a four-point harness to attach us to our seat. After our arrested landing at sea aboard the aircraft carrier we went to the Captain's elegant dining room for lunch. In the afternoon we watched a flight demonstration from the tower of the aircraft carrier. It was a memorable day for everyone aboard. When it was time for the COD to return to Subic Bay Naval Air Station I turned to Bud and said, "I'll stay with the wives who want to ride the aircraft carrier back into Subic Bay."

Bud looked at me in amazement and said, "No way, you go climb aboard that airplane and get a real catapult shot."

"Alright," I answered, knowing that I would prefer to stay in the luxurious Captain's quarters and ride the aircraft carrier into port. I also knew this was important to Bud so I went along with his suggestion. I sat in a steel seat facing backwards in the tunnel cabin of the C2-A aircraft. Again a young man assisted me in hooking up my four-point harness and adjusted my headset for sound suppression. I was quite relaxed until the pilot pushed the throttles to full power. The turbulence from the two propellers trying to launch as the aircraft was held back by the catapult caused us to shake all over. Then when the catapult fired I was thrust forward in the straps so violently I thought my head might possibly come off. The aircraft accelerated down the track and just as quickly was released from the catapult and we were flying in seconds. After I gathered my composure I wondered how I ever got the courage to do this. The answer of course was that I had done it for Bud, but was pleased and proud of my decision. My reward came several weeks later when a letter arrived by mail. I opened the envelope and inside was my official certificate designating me as a real, not honorary, *Tailhooker*.

The second trip was almost as thrilling as my landing and catapult shot aboard the *USS Midway*. When the aircraft carrier *Midway* went into a Navy shipyard for modification, the CTF-70 staff had the unprecedented opportunity to ride the battleship *USS New Jersey* during fleet operations. The Admiral arranged for a dependents cruise during which time the families from the senior staff were invited to ride aboard the *New Jersey* and watch an at-sea demonstration. It was a majestic day in all respects.

The *New Jersey*, along with several other World War II battleships, had been decommissioned in 1957. In 1967 she was taken out of mothballs and made fully combat ready. In 1968 she had been reactivated and modernized for service in Vietnam. During the war she played an active role firing her sixteen-inch shells from her huge gun turrets into enemy territory. She was decommissioned in 1969 but later recommissioned as part of President Reagan's six-hundred-ship Navy.

As the crew and CTF-70 staff cruised from Subic Bay to Manila we passed a small island that was designated as a target area. The *Jerseymen* crew manned the sixteen-inch gun turrets as we watched with sound protection on our ears as they fired a broadside. Bud explained, "A broadside is when the fore and aft gun turrets are fired simultaneously from the same side of the ship." The enormous boom and flash of fire from the turrets was followed by about a thirty-degree roll as the huge ship recoiled from the firepower. Maybe because I had attended so many flight demonstrations throughout the years, and had comparisons, I found our time aboard the magnificent battle ship *New Jersey* to be a once in a lifetime memory. How I would have loved to share the day with Sherri, Sue and two of my favorite girlfriends.

Before saying farewell to the Philippines Bud screened again for command as the Carrier Airwing Commander (Super CAG) aboard the *USS Constellation*. He would travel often with the Airwing and deployed on a six-month cruise. I continued to receive his flying adventures by mail. One story more than any previous one involved an accident he was involved in while he was the esteemed CAG. I wrote him of my regret at being unable to be with him and offer hands-on comfort and support.

Being married to a Navy carrier pilot requires countless sacrifices. Among the most difficult is the loneliness that comes from long separations. Bud and I would be separated for months at a time. Fortunately as a child I had learned to manage loneliness. Of course, I missed him terribly and at times yearned for his physical closeness, but through it all I felt a soul connection between us.

I did what I thought was important as a Navy wife but wasn't overly involved with luncheons or activities and avoided gossip whenever possible. I had been subjected to prejudice growing up and knew the harm caused by thoughtless remarks. As Bud's responsibilities in the Navy grew my involvement with the Naval Ombudsman program expanded. The Navy family was changing from the familiar traditional roles. Some families would make the difficult decision to not accompany a spouse to a new duty station. Instead, they would remain behind for various reasons. Sometimes it was due to schools for their children or the wife establishing a successful career.

Bud wisely used an old Indian proverb which says, "Let me not criticize another until I have walked a mile in his moccasins." It was more important to provide understanding and the ombudsman program opened lines of communication between the command and the family.

There was never an issue as to whether or not I would accompany him to his next duty station. Although there was the time after he received orders to CTF-70 in the Philippines that he was asked to leave me behind. I was successfully selling real estate in Lemoore and my broker and manager paid a visit to Bud and asked if I could stay in Lemoore after he deployed. They promised him that they would give me a guaranteed salary and visits to see him twice a year.

He just looked at them with his charming devilish smile, "I'm happy you ladies recognize my treasure. The extra money would be nice but the price is much too high for us to be separated unnecessarily for such a long period of time."

God, I love this man who came into my life and opened window after window to allow laughter, light and love to flow through.

25

Broken Habit Patterns

It was a late cloudy afternoon as the USS *Constellation* cruised in the Indian Ocean. I was scheduled for a day launch and night recovery in an F-14 Tomcat. As the Carrier Air Group Commander (CAG) I made sure I flew aircraft from each squadron in the Airwing and today I was flying with the VF-154 Black Knights. Lieutenant (Mean Jim) Greene would fly with me as my radar intercept officer (RIO). The aircraft was locked on catapult one and ready to take tension.

The F-14 Tomcat was passed from the yellow shirt over to the catapult officer. I watched the catapult officer survey the area on the flight deck surrounding the aircraft to make sure it was clear before looking up at me. With his right arm fully extended, and rapidly moving two fingers back and forth, he signaled for me to push the big F-14 Tomcat's throttles to full military power. I checked my gauges a final time and waited for the catapult officer's next command. I expected to see the catapult officer flashing his hand from an open fist to a closed one, a signal for me to go outboard and forward with the throttles and select zone five afterburner. Instead the Air Boss came up on the radio and said, "CAG, we're going to suspend you on catapult one."

The catapult officer immediately stepped directly in front of the F-14 on the catapult track. By stepping in front of the aircraft he communicated to me that the catapult had in fact been suspended and would not fire. I was proficient enough in the Tomcat to relax and reduce the throttles to idle. Suspending a launch once an aircraft was on the catapult doesn't happen often but was not unprecedented. Typically suspending a launch meant there was something wrong in the catapult launch sequence.

The residual thrust on the sixty thousand pound F-14 Tomcat at idle was quite high and tedious as I continued to hold the brakes. I selected the parking brake, allowing me to take my feet off the top of the rudder pedals I had been pushing to hold the brakes.

Just about the time I thought the launch would be scrubbed the Air Boss came up on the radio and said, "Okay, CAG, we are going to shoot you."

I keyed the intercom button on the throttle and said, "Mean Jim, they have broken our habit pattern, start over with the checklist!" Before every take-off and landing a pilot goes through a thorough checklist of the cockpit. In this case as we were ready to launch the cycle was broken. For safety of flight I had asked Mean Jim to start over with our take-off checklist.

All attention was focused on the catapult officer as he worked with the catapult crew to prepare for launch, as Mean Jim quickly repeated, "Wings, flaps, trim, controls" on his checklist. The catapult officer then swept his hands below his waist, signaling the catapult crew to take tension on the catapult. I could feel the aircraft crouch as the launch bar seated into the catapult track. The catapult officer looked directly at me sitting inside the cockpit of the F-14. Steam was streaming out of the catapult track as the catapult officer fully extended his right arm, waving his two fingers back and forth in the air signaling for me to go to full power. Instruments inside the cockpit were good and I looked down at the catapult officer, waiting for the afterburner signal. I received the signal right away. The catapult officer, with his arm extended, rapidly opened and closed his fist. I pushed outboard and forward with the big throttles and could feel all five zones of the afterburner stages kick in. Behind the aircraft were two very large cones of blue and yellow flames blasting against the jet blast deflector. Smoke and steam rose high into the sky as I crisply saluted the catapult officer. The salute was returned and the catapult officer gracefully dropped to one knee. He extended his arm, touched the flight deck and away we go!

Broken Habit Patterns

The first blast jammed Mean Jim's and my head back into the crotch of the ejection seat. My Radar Intercept Officer and I felt the acceleration continue rapidly throughout our abdomens as the g forces tempted me to pull the throttles aft. But the throttles were held firmly in place by my fingers wrapped over the steel catapult grip. And then, a BIG problem! First, the portside of the Tomcat dropped down with BOOM and then the starboard side. The aircraft continued its acceleration from zero to one hundred and fifty miles per hour in two and one-half seconds, where the F-14 was unimpeded by the apparent blowing of both tires. Both wheels had been locked by the parking break, and did not slow the big jet down by a knot.

Back on the flight deck huge pieces of rubber flew aft down the flight deck as the tires disintegrated. The launch continued with metal rims screeching along the steel flight deck. The Air Boss came up on the radio just as the Tomcat lifted off the bow and said, "Don't raise your gear CAG; you have blown both tires!"

"No shit!" I muttered to myself and said aloud, "Roger that." I came out of afterburner, raised the flaps and pointed the F-14 away from the aircraft carrier. I remained below six hundred feet to avoid aircraft entering the break to land back aboard aircraft carrier.

The cockpit was unusually quiet for a very long time. I was embarrassed and upset that I had taken a catapult shot with the parking brake on. I was also royally pissed off at Mean Jim for not checking when I said, "Mean Jim, they have broken our habit pattern; start over with the checklist." Unfortunately, he started the checklist right below the parking brake. I would deal with my anger later, because now I had a major emergency situation to handle.

There are a lot of hydraulic fuel lines and electrical connections in the wheel well of the Tomcat. Occasionally when an aircraft launched with the parking brakes on several large chunks of hot rubber from the blown tires had been thrown into the hydraulic lines. The pilot doesn't raise the landing gear because pieces of hot, burning rubber could be trapped inside the wheel well and cause a fire once the gear was raised. Often a hydraulic failure resulted in a pilot ejecting from the aircraft.

Fortunately, in my case, none of the additional challenges happened. However, Mean Jim and I still faced several risks. The Air Boss directed me to climb overhead the carrier and hold until all returning aircraft were recovered aboard the aircraft carrier. One anomaly of the F-14 Tomcat was the pilot could not dump fuel with the landing gear extended. The aircraft launched with sixteen thousand pounds of fuel but maximum fuel for landing was six thousand pounds. I had to get rid of ten thousand pounds of jet fuel, or one thousand five hundred gallons, and was unable to dump with my wheels extended. I also needed to get rid of my fuel within thirty minutes. My only option was to select afterburner. I pointed the nose of the F-14 up about thirty degrees to allow for a very high burn rate without accelerating above the one hundred and eighty knot landing gear limit.

After all aircraft in the returning event had landed aboard the *Connie* I was directed to set up for a straight-in approach. I lowered the flaps and tailhook and approached the carrier from three miles out. I flew a nice pass keeping the yellow *meatball* centered between the green datum lights on the Fresnel lens all the way in. At three-quarter mile I keyed the mike and said, "105 Tomcat ball."

The LSO responded, "Roger ball, you're looking good."

I eased the big jet down to the flight deck as I normally would when landing aboard the aircraft carrier. This time the Tomcat slammed down hard and the landing was much more violent than usual. With no rubber on the wheels, the rims impacted the metal flight deck with an enormous bang at four hundred feet per minute. The nose wheels of the big Tomcat made forceful contact with the flight deck. The tailhook engaged the number three wire. I pushed the throttles to one hundred percent, causing the aircraft to come to a violent stop. I was nearly knocked unconscious by the hard landing and was at full power with the F-14 leaning significantly to starboard when the aircraft stopped. I pulled the throttle to idle and regained my bearings. The Tomcat leaning starboard caused the right wing tip to nearly touch the flight deck. The crash crew raced toward the damaged F-14. Once the appropriate safety pins were put into place the yellow shirts signaled for me to secure the engines.

As I opened the canopy I felt the cool breeze fill the cockpit of the Tomcat. Steam from the bow catapults was blowing past and gave me the opportunity to reflect on my embarrassment. Here I was the heralded CAG, the pilot that every pilot dreamed of becoming. My wrecked jet was sitting sideways on the flight deck and broken because I "*fucked up*"! I was the CAG who had my name on both side of the cockpit of nine aircraft in the airwing. Captain Bud Orr, CAG was painted on each side of every aircraft with 00 on it. There were two F-14s, number 100 and 200, two A-7s, number 300 and 400, one A-6E, number 500, one EA-6B, number 600, one E-2, number 700 and the helicopter was number 900. A bit heady, but oh so cool!

A few years later when I was a lobbyist for Rolls-Royce in Washington, D.C., a friend called to say he had seen a plastic model kit for sale in a store in the Crystal City Mall in Arlington, Virginia. The model was of an FA-18C Hornet with a picture on the box that had the paint job for the CAG bird on a VFA-113 aircraft with the name Captain Bud Orr, CAG on the box and also on the decal for the model. "Wow," I thought, "I have been immortalized by the Japanese."

The VF-154 maintenance crew arrived and jacked up the aircraft. They ran a start cart with a mattress on top under the starboard wing to allow the big Tomcat to be cleared from the landing area. I wanted to be invisible as the aircraft was slowly towed to the aircraft elevator where we would be lowered to the hangar deck for repair of the collapsed starboard landing gear. In twenty-two years of flying I had never seriously damaged a Navy aircraft airframe, and now as the CAG I had done it in living color in front of five thousand men on the *USS Constellation*. The experience was extremely humbling.

The maintenance effort that followed was extensive. In order to access the area inside the wing where the starboard landing gear collapsed the maintenance personnel had to cut a hole in the starboard wheel well. I looked back during the repair made by the maintenance crew to a few months earlier in the cruise to understand a stunt that was pulled on me.

The *USS Constellation* had steamed toward the West Coast of Australia where the carrier would enter port at Perth for an eight day liberty call. In advance of the port visit the airwing requested and received clearance from the City of Perth to make a formation flyover the city. I led the flyover, consisting of eight F-14 Tomcats, eight A-7 Corsair IIs, four A-6 Intruders and two EA-6B Hawkeyes flying in a wedge formation. The airwing flew over the city at eight hundred feet with thousands of residents cheering in the streets. When the airwing recovered aircraft aboard the carrier the Admiral called me up to his cabin. I was reprimanded for leaflets which had been dropped over Perth by one of the aircraft. The leaflets invited the local women to attend the VF-154 Black Knights party and included a map providing date, time and location to the party.

Love at First Flight

Enraged, I called the Commanding Officer of the VF-154 Black Knights, whose call sign was Meatball, to my cabin. I told the Skipper he had violated Navy regulations regarding dropping anything from a military aircraft, let alone during a flyover. Meatball had allowed his squadron to stash the invitations in the speed brake of one of the F-14 Tomcats. The pilot opened the speed brake over Perth, spreading invitations out over the city. For his punishment I put the Skipper in hack, restricted aboard the ship, for the first two nights of liberty in Perth.

After my incident with the F-14 Tomcat, in retaliation the VF-154 Black Knight's Commanding Officer, Meatball, allowed or possibly directed his maintenance people to perform a petty, vindictive act. The maintenance aircrew repaired the damage to the F-14 and sealed up the hole. The aircrew then cut a piece of sheet metal into the rectangular shape of a large band-aid and detailed it to look like a real band-aid. Next, the crew stenciled *CAG-AID* next to the patch. The Tomcat was parked on the hanger bay for weeks, in a place where anyone passing by would not miss the subtle pun. I could have ordered the patch and CAG-AID to be removed from the Tomcat but felt perhaps this was the price I had to pay for damaging an aircraft in front of my airwing.

26

Alpha Papa

Along with loving my aviator I vicariously experienced joy and happiness over his achievements and on occasion felt the heartbreak of his disappointments. Through it all I learned a great deal about my husband and the way the Navy functions. I gained personal insights into the men Bud worked for and the men and women who worked for him. In the totality of his Navy career one event stands alone for testing his strength under fire and also his ability to face isolation and suffer alone. He was on cruise when a tragic accident occurred and was unable to share the story in its entirety until he returned home.

Historically in the Naval Aviation community, the Captain of an aircraft carrier was the preeminent ranking officer. All ship's company personnel reported to the Captain through the department heads. In addition to ship's company, the Carrier Airwing Group Commander (CAG) was viewed as one of the Captain's department heads.

There are approximately five thousand men on an aircraft carrier, roughly half of the men are ship's company and the other half made up the airwing and report to the Carrier Airwing Group Commander.

In October 1983, U.S. forces invaded Grenada. In the wake of a military coup, code name Operation Urgent Fury ousted a revolutionary government. The top two commanders leading the invasion were Admiral Joseph Metcalf III, the Commander of Second Fleet, and his Deputy

Commander Major General H. Norman Schwarzkopf. A review of the operation under the leadership of then Secretary of the Navy John Lehman identified several major shortcomings.

First, strike planning and the subsequent execution appeared flawed and undisciplined. This prompted President Reagan's administration spokesman Larry Speakes and Alan Berger from the *Boston Globe* both to report on the same day, "Grenada was a floating craps game and we didn't know who was in charge." The other major shortcoming was the lack of leadership by the Carrier Air Wing Commander aboard the aircraft carrier. His leadership was deemed to have been less than ideal. Lessons learned from the invasion prompted Secretary Lehman to institutionalize two unprecedented initiatives. Under his direction the Naval Aviation Strike Warfare Center was established. Naval Air Station Fallon, Nevada, was selected as the ideal site for the new graduate-level university for teaching and institutionalizing modern strike warfare planning and tactics. Establishment of the Strike Warfare Center was afforded top funding and manning priority by the Navy and Congress. This meant no cost was spared and the very best people were selected to stand up the Strike Warfare Center.

Captain Joe Prueher flew the A-6 Intruder. He was a rising young military star, Naval Academy graduate, Vietnam combat veteran and former Airwing Commander. He was personally selected by Secretary Lehman to be the first Commanding Officer of the Strike Warfare Center. Under Captain Prueher's astute leadership a framework was designed for the most highly technical and strategic planning institution Naval Aviation had ever known. Only the smartest and best pilots and aircrews received orders to create the model.

Today the Strike Warfare Center continues as the center of gravity for all Naval Aviation graduate level training in planning and execution of Carrier Battle Group Tactics. Captain Prueher demonstrated his intellect and strategic leadership and went on to retire as a four-star admiral as the Senior U.S. Military Commander in the Pacific and Indian Ocean. After retiring he was appointed by President Bush as the U.S. Ambassador to the People's Republic of China.

A second but equally revolutionary initiative by Secretary Lehman resulted in the creation of the *Super CAG* program, as the initiative was colloquially branded. No longer would the Carrier Airwing Group Commander continue

Alpha Papa

as a department head reporting to the Captain of the aircraft carrier. The new senior CAG would be an 0-6 Captain, rather than a 0-5 Commander, and was equal to the Captain of the aircraft carrier rather than reporting to him. Both Captains aboard the aircraft carrier would report to the Battle Group Commander. The Battle Group Commander was the Admiral. He was headquartered aboard the aircraft carrier and was responsible for all Battle Group Warfare executions. Both programs inspired by Secretary Lehman's vision have successfully matured over the years.

After Bud's tour as the Operations Officer for Carrier Task Force Seventy, CTF-70, in the Philippines, he was selected to be the first senior CAG (Super CAG) aboard the *USS Constellation*. He was honored to follow in the footsteps of Captain (Zap) Zlatopher aboard the *USS Enterprise* and Captain (Bad Fred) Lewis aboard the *USS Eisenhower*, the first Super CAGs who served concurrently.

Bud trained for a full year before becoming the Super CAG. He attended highly classified Pentagon briefings and met with senior flag officers and various specialty schools, including anti-submarine warfare and special operations. To him, the most attractive part of the job was the opportunity to have command of nine squadrons with six different types of fixed wing aircraft, as well as two helicopter squadrons, all of which he flew.

As previously mentioned I trained to fly the F-14 Tomcat and FA-18 Hornet both day and night aboard the carrier. I also flew the A-6 Intruder, S-3 Viking, EA6-B Prowler and the E-2 Hawkeye from the ship in the daytime as well as taking off and landing at various naval air stations. Because of my experience and ability flying the Harrier and the training I received, I also flew three types of helicopters off the carrier.

Having command and flying various aircraft was the best part of being the CAG. The serious part was being one of the five Captains who made up the Warfare Commander Staff reporting to the Battle Group Commander.

The overall Battle Group Commander was the Composite Warfare Commander (CWC) who acted as the central command authority for the entire Battle Group. Within the Battle Group, the CWC could best control combat operations from the aircraft carrier. Each of the Warfare Commanders were tasked with defensive operations to protect the Battle Group, except for (Alpha Papa) Strike Warfare. The Strike Warfare Commander was the CAG, and in that position I was accountable for all resources capable of projection of power ashore or at sea. Torpedoes from submarines, missiles launched from submarines or ships to strike targets, and air-to-air and air-to-ground weapons capable of striking targets at sea or shore were under my accountability. This was part of the Secretary Lehman's revolution which provided cohesive leadership to take responsibility for protection of the Battle Group with its organic capability to project power ashore or at sea.

During workups leading up to deployment, the Battle Group and Airwing leadership spent many hours briefing and planning for a major exercise to be conducted in the Hawaiian Operations area as we transited through en route to the Indian Ocean. There were multiple exercises that would test the capabilities of each of the Warfare Commanders and the accountable resources included a range of enemy forces *Orange Air* directed by the Third Fleet Commander headquartered in Hawaii. U.S. submarines posing as enemy attempted simulated strikes on the Battle Group. U.S. surface ships attempted to penetrate the perimeter of the Battle Group and multiple air-to-air missile strikes were planned against drones to exercise the fighter's air-to-air competence.

Rather than projection of power ashore, a war-at-sea evolution was staged for the Airwing to demonstrate coordinated Battle Group tactics. The target ship was a retired U.S. Navy surface ship, filled with Styrofoam to assist in flotation while under attack from real weapons. At the appropriate time as directed by the Third Fleet Commander, the target ship was towed out from a Hawaiian island at the briefed latitude and longitude where the ship would inevitably be relocated by Airwing assets and identified as a threat to the Battle Group. To make the exercise more complex and challenging for Alpha Papa (CAG) was the simultaneous strike of three Harpoon missiles, one each from a submarine, a surface ship and an FA-18 Hornet. This also happened to be the first time an FA-18 had delivered a Harpoon missile outside of the test and evaluation environment.

The night before the planned strike, the Operations Department of the Third Fleet Commander based in Hawaii ***allegedly*** messaged the E-2 squadron ready room that the coordinates of the target ship had changed. The ship had been dropped off under tow to a different location than previously briefed. Regrettably, the E-2 squadron had no record of this reported change. The first E-2 launched from the flight deck of the *Constellation* at 0200 in the morning and began the surface search to develop the surface plot. This plot identified all surface vessels within a hundred miles of the aircraft carrier and the information was sent electronically back to the ships operations center. In the surface plot there was a contact *exactly* where the target ship was supposed to have been based upon the coordinates the E-2 squadron had been briefed it would be. At 0600 the E-2 crew was relieved by another E-2 crew and the surface plot was electronically transferred from one to the other with the target clearly marked.

That morning I led a flight of four F-14s on an early launch as the observer for a competitive Sidewinder shoot, the same event that launched the *war at sea* strike against the unknown enemy ship which was also scheduled to be attacked by the three Harpoon missiles. The F-18s were vectored by the E-2 to the target ship. The Harpoons from the submarine and destroyer got their targeting from a separate source.

After the AIM-9 missile exercise I led the four Tomcats back to the *Connie* for recovery. I landed aboard and taxied to a parking spot on the stern, shut down the engines and climbed out of the cockpit. I was always happy to return from an exciting and successful flight.

As I strode back toward the tower I saw someone running aft on the flight deck toward me. As the figure approached I could see it was Christine Fox, the beautiful blond exercise analyst attached to the Third Fleet in Hawaii. She had been on the Top Gun Staff in San Diego when the movie *Top Gun* was filmed and her role in the movie was cast by Kelly McGillis.

As she continued to stride toward me I began to have a bad feeling. We almost collided as she pulled my helmet close so she could talk over the noise of jet engines. I will never forget the moment she said, "CAG, the Airwing had a Harpoon missile hit a civilian ship!" The accident changed my life forever.

As we walked back into Strike Operations there was a calamitous atmosphere. When the dust settled the story was clear. An Indian container ship had been struck by a Harpoon missile. Even though the missile was a training missile with no warhead, the missile penetrated the ship's superstructure. The missile crashed through a window in the bridge and exited the back, leaving about a ten-inch hole, carrying the Philippine radioman with it.

The ensuing investigation was lengthy and painful. The inquiries continued during the Indian Ocean cruise and throughout the remainder of the Battle Group's transit up the West Coast into Canada and Alaska. We returned to San Diego before the official record was released. The final completion of the investigation occurred after my Change of Command as CAG. I knew the report would not be like putting lipstick on a pig. I also realized it was more important that I not let my young pilots see the stress I was enduring.

I had a wonderful large stateroom with private bedroom and bathroom aboard the ship. I spent my days flying several kinds of aircraft in the Airwing and up very late at night responding to the never-ending inquisitions into the accident. I was exhausted and emotional, but when I put on my flight gear, briefed with the young aircrews and flew with them I always attempted to project a positive front. I wanted them to aspire to and have the opportunity to become the illustrious Super CAG. More than anything I wanted them to have the best job in the world, and never see the toll the accident was taking on me physically and personally.

When the investigation was complete I was found to be accountable because as Super CAG (Alpha Papa) the Strike Warfare Commander was in charge of the strike. I believe that command in the Navy is about accountability. If the Captain of the ship runs the ship aground he is relieved, no questions. I accept and agree the process is proper.

The accident investigation was reviewed in the Pentagon by the Vice Chief of Naval Operations, Admiral Stan Arthur. He sent the report back to be redone, claiming that the Three Star Admiral, Commander of the Third Fleet was also causal. The admiral and I were awarded non-punitive letters of reprimand. The letter I received was not made a part of my permanent service record, that is, *non-punitive*. The label did not change the reality. The highly visible accident was known throughout the fleet.

After the Change of Command I was detailed to the prestigious assignment as Principle Deputy of Senate Liaison in Washington, D.C. When it came time for selection to Admiral, my name was not on the list. Who knows why? I may never know the reason, although I had given the selection board a

Alpha Papa

good reason not to promote me. I haven't looked back. I know that we cannot change the past and the most tragic moment of my career.

During the accident investigation I received overseas telephone calls often from Bud. He called from the ship asking me to call several of the airwing wives whose husbands were involved in the accident. He was always complimentary of the pilots and wanted me to convey how proud he was of the men under his command at the airwing wives' functions.

He said, "Franny, be sure to call and tell the wife whose husband shot the harpoon missile through the Indian container ship he is doing well and how proud I am of him and all the men in the Airwing. Most of all tell her not to worry about any rumors involving her husband and the accident." In retrospect, I think one of the reasons Bud showed such strength and was able to keep a positive attitude throughout this difficult time was due to his ability to look for and find joy moment by moment.

The squadron Commanding Officer of the FA-18 squadron whose pilot fired the Harpoon made Admiral before he retired. The pilot who fired the Harpoon was selected to command a squadron and made Captain. Bud made sure no one below him paid a price for the accident!

Just as Bud wanted me to shelter the wives in the Airwing from the emotional uncertainty of the accident, he was also protecting me. I did not realize until several years later the depth of his suffering. I had married him for love, without a condition he become an Admiral. The incredible man I married has never disappointed me. He is affectionate, gregarious, complicated and oh so much fun. I held him in my arms when he told me his father cried when he learned that he did not make Admiral. I know his father's tears brought him the greatest pain. I love a man that throughout his life has taken the time to get to know the people who work for him and has helped so many who have crossed his path. I wanted adventure and luckily adventure found me on a blind date.

27
Another Notch in My Pistol

I RETURNED FROM A SIX-MONTH CRUISE in the Western Pacific and Indian Ocean in 1989 as the Carrier Air Group Commander (CAG) aboard the *USS Constellation*. Extensive carrier Battle Group training was required when preparing the aircraft carrier and airwing for the next cruise. The *USS Constellation*, Airwing Fourteen and several surface ships departed San Diego for the Battle Group exercises. During transit the task force cruised up the Pacific coast toward Alaska and was attacked by the simulated enemy, *Orange Air*. The *Orange Air* land-based aircraft attacked the Battle Group as they fought their way up the West Coast, executing strikes into the Fallon, Nevada, weapons complex. Initially the simulated enemy was a combination of U.S. Air Force and U.S. Navy aircraft. Once we crossed the Canadian border our aircrews made simulated strikes into Canada and were attacked by Royal Canadian FA-18 Hornets.

One significant strike I led during the exercise was a flight of four F-14 Tomcats flying low level through the Canadian Rockies. We flew well below the mountaintops and were intercepted by Canadian F-18 Hornets diving on us from the tops of the Rockies. The attack culminated in dogfights throughout the valleys. The Canadians were exceptional pilots and adversaries throughout the exercise.

Love at First Flight

Once the Battle Group reached the Alaskan coastline they came under simulated attack day and night from U.S. Air Force fighters and a B-1 bomber out of Elmendorf, Alaska. The B-1 Lancer was unusually successful making its way low level at a relative speed of three hundred and sixty miles per hour across the Pacific. The aircraft got very close to the *Connie* before being detected on radar by the Aegis Cruiser, which was the main line of defense for the carrier battle group.

At the completion of the exercise the Third Fleet Commander and the Captain of the Aegis Cruiser were flown by helicopter from his ship to the *USS Constellation,* where we met on the aircraft carrier. After a brief meeting the three of us flew from the carrier aboard a C-2 Carrier Onboard Delivery aircraft into Elmendorf Air Force Base to debrief the exercise. Representatives of the battle group and *Orange Air,* the simulated enemy forces, attended the meeting. Each team explained their role in the exercise and the perceived success or failure. The inputs from the teams either corroborated or contradicted the other team's perceptions. All inputs were recorded for the "*Battle Group Report for Action.*"

One of the most remarkable flaws in the battle group defenses was the failure of the Aegis Cruiser radar to detect the B-1 bomber as it attacked the battle group at two hundred and fifty knots or two hundred and ninety miles per hour and two hundred feet above the water. The B-1 could put the wing of the aircraft back at two hundred and fifty knots and the radar cross section on the Aegis Cruiser would appear about the size of an F-16 Falcon, a very small target on the ship's radar. The reason for the low detection rate was because of the stealth characteristics built into the aircraft. The Battle Group staff projected the stealth problem to the worst case with the B-1 bomber attacking the battle group at Mach 1.2 or over six hundred miles per hour rather than ambling in at two hundred and fifty knots. The ability of the secret design produced a weak radar return and the results showed an even more critical shortcoming in the Battle Group's defenses.

After the debrief I went to the Officer's Club for a beer. *Can you imagine that?* Three officers in U.S. Air Force flight suits were sitting at a table and I asked if I could join them. The pilots just happened to be the B-1 crew. After spending time with them and enjoying a bit of tactics talk I said, "Hey, how would you like to fly out to the *Connie* with me tomorrow and fly in our airwing aircraft?"

Stunned and excited by the prospect and the opportunity one of them said, "Can you do that as a 0-6?" What he meant was did I have the authority to authorize them to fly airwing aircraft as a Navy Captain and Airwing Commander?

I said, "Of course, they're my jets."

The next day the pilots received clearance from their Commanding Officer that allowed them to fly with the Airwing. The B-1 bomber crew was given cold weather *poopy suits* to wear on the flight out to the aircraft carrier aboard the COD. I knew they hated wearing the cold weather gear, but it was necessary in these sea water temperatures. However, their excitement kept them from making comments. Carrier Airwing Fourteen flew the Air Force aircrew in various multi-seat aircraft and each of them got two catapult shots and two carrier landings. The aircrew flew in the EA-6B, E2-C Hawkeye, S-3 Viking or the F-14 Tomcat. After their flights they were flown back to Elmendorf, Alaska, in the Carrier Onboard Delivery aircraft before returning to their home base at McConnell Air Force Base in Wichita, Kansas.

Following the exercise *Constellation* steamed back into San Diego. I received an incredible message from the Commander of the Strategic Air Command (CINCSAC), a four-star U.S. Air Force General. The message read, "*Captain Bud Orr is authorized to fly the B-1 bomber at the McConnell Air Force Base in Wichita, Kansas.*" McConnell Air Force Base was the home base of the B-1 Lancer crew I had brought aboard the *USS Constellation*.

"Bud, did this really come as a surprise to you?" Fran asked.

"Fran, it was truly unprecedented and hard to believe that I was going to get to fly the B-1. I knew there was a long list of generals in Washington, D.C., waiting their turn to fly the aircraft and I went to the top of the list!"

Upon departing the *Connie* and returning to Miramar Naval Air Station in San Diego I made arrangements for the flight to McConnell Air Force Base. I spoke with the U.S. Air Force Wing Commander whose aircraft I would fly and was informed that my copilot and two mission specialists would be none other than the same B-1 aircrew I had met in the Officer's Club in Elmendorf, Alaska.

I invited two junior officers, one from each FA-18 Hornet squadron in Carrier Airwing Fourteen, to join me. I flew an F-14 Tomcat with my Radar Intercept Officer (RIO); the two Hornets pilots were Greg (Shifty) Peairs and

Love at First Flight

Tommy (Trots) Trotter, who flew from Naval Air Station Lemoore, California, to meet me at the Miramar Naval Air Station in San Diego. Shifty, Trots and I joined up and continued to McConnell Air Force Base where we were met by the B-1 Wing Commander and my new Air Force friends.

The Commanding Officer of the B-1 squadron and I went out to the flight line for my cockpit checkout in preparation for my flight the following day. Since there wasn't a simulator or trainer for the B-1 bomber, the Commanding Officer got into the right seat and I climbed into the left seat. We spent about an hour on my checkout. Later in the afternoon the CO and I joined Shifty and Trots for dinner at the Officer's Club. It was early to bed in preparation for the exciting and stimulating day ahead of us.

The next morning, my aircrew and I briefed the mission in the hanger before the exciting flight. The B-1 bomber flight would include the take-off and climb to altitude toward the Northwest into a restricted area to rendezvous with Shifty and Trots in the FA-18 Hornets for radar intercept training.

"Hold up just a second. What is intercept training?" Fran asked.

"Intercept training is an important warfare specialty in carrier aviation which ensures the carrier is not threatened and will still be there when air crews return from their missions. It is a highly sophisticated radar system linked to the aircraft's weapons that allow early detection and destruction of a threat to the aircraft carrier. Radar intercept training provides aircrews with detection, tracking and simulated attacks on aircraft acting as potential threats."

After completing radar intercept training we would detach from the Hornets and enter a low-level training track and fly farther north into Nebraska and South Dakota. We would fly at two hundred feet above ground, at three hundred and fifty knots or over four hundred miles per hour, some of the time was actually *hands off*. We briefed following the low level that I would pilot the B-1 back into a restricted area and rendezvous with a KC-135 in-flight refueling tanker and practice tanking from the *boom* before returning to McConnell Air Force Base for practice landings.

After completing the brief in the hangar my copilot and the two mission specialists and I walked out of the hangar into the majestic, cool, spring morning and approached the flight line. I advanced deferentially toward the huge one hundred and eighty thousand pound jet aircraft filled with another one hundred and eighty thousand pounds of fuel.

"Sorry to interrupt again, but the fuel weighed the same as the B-1?" Fran asked.

"You do keep me on my toes, my love. The answer is yes!"

The three hundred and sixty thousand pound dark green beauty, with its long pointed nose and itinerant canard and grand swept and movable wings looked like it was going Mach 2 just sitting on the ramp. I had the familiar rush of butterflies in my stomach as I walked around the aircraft to pre-flight in anticipation, knowing I would soon be piloting this magnificent jet.

The crew climbed into their respective seats. I was in the front left or captain seat, my copilot was to my right. The two mission specialists, one for offensive systems and the other for defensive systems, climbed into their stations in the back of the aircraft.

I followed the Commanding Officer's instructions on which I had been carefully briefed. I strapped in and located the large black start button in the middle of the console. The aircraft was designed as a Strategic Air Command nuclear bomber and the aircrews at various times had stood SAC alert sitting in the cockpit. Timing was critical if the aircraft were to be ordered to execute a nuclear strike mission. The startup time on four engines would be excessive. A brilliant engineer designed a system that allowed the pilot to start all four engines at one time by simply banging a button. The big black button in the cockpit looked much like a Staples *Easy* button. With concurrence from the copilot and upon the start signal from the plane captain standing on the ramp in front of the aircraft I banged the big button. Like magic all four engines came alive at the same time.

Next was the routine plane captain's check list of flight controls, followed by the removal of all tie down chains and safety pins, and the aircraft was ready to taxi down the runway. The copilot managed radio communications and all I had to do was taxi out to the end of the runway and take off. One feature on the B-1 bomber that was new for me was the manual wing sweep lever. The F-14 Tomcat with the variable sweep wing could be put into auto mode. In auto mode the aircraft would adjust the wing sweep to optimize the airspeed and angle of attack automatically. However, the B-1 was not a fighter. It was a high-speed bomber and the pilot would manually select the wing sweep based upon the airspeed at the time. With clearance for take-off from the tower I taxied to the center of the runway, released the brakes and smoothly pushed all four engines to military, one hundred percent power and the B-1 was quickly airborne.

The flight went just as we briefed. The aircraft flew like a small fighter at high speed and a big lumbering jet at low speed. Radar intercept work with the F-18 Hornets proceeded well and we descended down into the low-level training route. The only time the copilot ever touched the stick in over six hours of flight time was to check out the automatic flight control system to allow the B-1 to fly hands-off at low level. Once the copilot's check out was complete, I engaged a few switches and let go.

There we were, zooming along at two hundred feet above the ground at over four hundred miles per hour like we were sitting in our living room. The aircraft climbed and descended smoothly to maintain two hundred feet above the undulating terrain. I admired the aerodynamics of this magnificent jet as we cruised along hands-off. I noted there was a slight but smooth rocking motion as the nose would move gently up and down. I attributed the rocking motion to the very long distance between the nose of the aircraft and the root of the wing. I also thought that might have been the reason for the canard design to the nose of the aircraft. A canard was a small set of aerodynamic wings mounted forward of the cockpit in the nose of the aircraft. Canards are very common in French fighters, but the B-1 is the only U.S. aircraft I was aware of that employed them. Perhaps the canards were required to minimize the small pitching motion I observed.

The low-level flight was completed and we climbed back up into the restricted area and rendezvoused with a KC-135 tanker. The KC-135 tanker was a very large airliner-sized aircraft flown during the Eisenhower years. The tanker had been designed and built during the Cold War to support massive tanking requirements for the B-52 bomber if it were to be actually employed in a nuclear mission.

There are two types of in-flight refueling used by U.S. military aircraft. The Navy uses *probe and drogue*. A tanker deploys a hose from the aircraft with a soft basket attached at the end of the hose. The Navy fighter has a *probe* which is either externally mounted or flush mounted and hydraulically extended by the pilot. The pilot positions his aircraft behind the tanker and approaches the *drogue* and lines up. Once stabilized he slowly approaches the *drogue*, maneuvering the aircraft so he is in position to thrust the *probe* into the center of the basket. Making contact he slowly pushes the basket in until reaching a safe refueling distance. He stabilizes his aircraft and the tanker pilot initiates refueling. When refueling is complete the pilot backs the aircraft out, uncouples from the *drogue* and moves clear so another aircraft can refuel.

"How fast were the planes flying when they refueled?" Fran asked.

"The aircraft are flying roughly between two hundred and thirty miles per hour to two hundred and seventy miles per hour. I know that sounds fast, but you must put yourself in the cockpit to appreciate the challenges that relate to the speed of the tanking aircraft. As the tanker and fleet aircraft are well above fifteen thousand feet and flying at the same airspeed, the speed is irrelevant. What matters is the closure rate between tanking aircraft and the tanker. Once the tanking aircraft stabilizes behind the *drogue,* which is at the end of a long hose from the tanker, the skill resides in the pilot who is tanking managing his closure rate with the *drogue* to allow him to get his *probe* into the drogue accurately without over- or undershooting."

The United States Air Force in-flight refueling procedure is totally different. The Air Force uses a very large tanker aircraft where a *boom operator* lies on a pad in the stern of the aircraft looking out a small window. He has control of the *boom,* which is a long tube that attaches under the aircraft when not in use. When the *boom* is released it hangs at about a thirty-degree angle below the aircraft with small bird-like fins that the *boom operator* employs to maneuver it. The pilot of the refueling aircraft flies formation under the tail of the large tanker and the *boom operator* maneuvers the *boom* over the nose of the fighter and then lowers it into the receptacle on the aircraft.

Although I made only practice plug-ins (meaning no gas was actually passed) to the B-1 bomber, I plugged and unplugged several times before detaching from the tanker. In retrospect, this was an excellent opportunity as I had wondered which refueling was the most difficult, the USAF *boom* or the U.S. Navy *probe and drogue*. I concluded that the *boom* was significantly less challenging from a pilot perspective.

The B-1 crew and I returned to Ellsworth for practice landings. As I was in the captain seat (the left seat) and the landing pattern was a right-hand approach for the day, landing was more difficult. I flew down the runway at four hundred knots or four hundred and sixty-four miles per hour and made a right-hand break. I turned downwind and slowed to approach speed as I lowered the landing gear and flaps and made sure the wings were fully extended. After passing the one-hundred-and-eighty-degree position abeam of the landing area at six hundred feet I started a right turn toward the runway. It was particularly difficult because I was looking across the large cockpit and through the right-hand canopy with the copilot in the foreground. Unfettered, I cranked it around to a perfect lineup down the center of the runway and flew the angle of attack all the way to touchdown.

When we touched down I heard the most horrific rumbling and clatter which frightened me, and I immediately pushed the throttles up to full power. My copilot said, "You were doing great. Why did you rush your take-off?"

I responded. "There was so much noise and clatter I thought the gear wasn't down or I had landed short."

The copilot instructor laughed aloud. He realized that I was not used to having ten wheels engage the runway with all of the moving parts and noise that occurred along the way. My next three touch and go's were much easier and my final landing was met with applause from the crew.

The departure and good-byes were quick. I thanked the B-1 crew and the Commanding Officer of the squadron for such a wonderful opportunity and jumped into the F-14 Tomcat with my RIO and prepared for take-off. The F-14 had always seemed like a huge aircraft to me compared to all the smaller single-seat fighters I had flown. Now the F-14 suddenly felt like a toy in comparison to the B-1. I taxied out to the end of the runway and waved to my colleagues standing on the porch of the small cabin in front of air operations. I asked for and received clearance for an *unrestricted climb*, and pushed the throttles up pass military power and into zone five afterburner. I zorched past the front porch with flames coming out of my ass, offered a final wave to my friends, pointed the jet straight up as I climbed to my assigned altitude and leveled off for my return to Miramar Naval Air Station in San Diego, California. Another welcomed notch in my pistol!

28
Presidential Commission

Silhouetted against Quaker Pond in the waning light of day Bud stood with his head down and hands in his pockets, deep in thought. Since the sad passing of Boo-Dog to old age, his ever-present blond cocker spaniel, Fallon, sat patiently by his side. Sensing me watching him Bud lifted his head, smiled and began the short walk home.

My real estate career was successful and my earnings helped us build a new forty-five-hundred-square-foot home in the City of Alexandria. Bud was proud of my success and at one of our frequent dinner parties embarrassed me by bragging on my multiple talents. I sometimes thought he believed I could do anything I sat my mind to accomplishing. Following his tour in the U.S. Senate as the Principle Deputy in the Office of Legislative Affairs his career in the Navy was coming to a close. He needed to decide what he wanted to do next. I remained supportive of whatever decision he made and was optimistic about the future.

His good friend Chris Paul, who was the Military Legislative Assistant to Senator John McCain, told him the Senator had been asked for nominations to a Presidential Commission under President George W. Bush. The commission was to be called the *Presidential Commission on the Assignment of Women in Combat.* Bud and I discussed the matter and thought the opportunity fascinating. He was excited about the experiences he would face and decided it would be a nice transition to civilian life should he be selected. He met with Chris and said, "I'm willing to give it a try, so toss my name into the ring."

Within a month I was invited to interview with the Presidential Employment Office in the Old Executive Building. The interview was conducted by the head of the office and two of her assistants. I was asked to brief them on my Navy career, provide personal background information and comment on whether I had any predisposition either for or against women in combat.

A week later I was recalled for an appointment and met only with the head of the office. She said, "Captain Orr, we were pleased with our initial interview and would like to know if you would be interested in taking the position as Staff Director of the Presidential Commission?" Without reservation, I accepted. The subject matter was one of international interest and as the director I would be exposed to the spectrum of opinions. I also felt my masters in Guidance and Counseling would be useful.

When Chris Paul had previously described the position he said, "The Commissioners and the Staff Director would be Executive Level-5." Executive Level-5 was one above Senior Executive Service-5 and was the equivalent of a two- to three-star general or admiral, with an annual salary of about one hundred and eight thousand dollars annually. This was a little heady to go from Captain to the equivalent of an admiral, but I felt ready to take on the challenge.

My first duty after accepting the position was to pay a call on the Director of Government Services Agency (GSA). He would provide service to the commission in the form of office space, furniture, supplies and administer all pay and allowances of commissioners and staff. My next two responsibilities were to find sufficient office space downtown and hire a competent staff.

It was also necessary for me to pay a call on my new boss, Chairman of the Commission General Robert Herres. General Herres was the Chief Executive Officer of USAA and had retired as a four-star General from the United States

Air Force. He had an illustrious career as a pilot, was the first Hispanic to be selected to Brigadier General in the Air Force and in his last position on active duty had been the first Vice Chairman of the Joint Chiefs of Staff. General Herres showed little emotion or warmth towards me or the staff. Instead, he was very direct and to the point. His first question to me was, "Why in the hell would you want this job?"

In retrospect, I wish I had asked the same question of the General. But of course I didn't. Instead I said, "I think the Commission will be an interesting and excellent transition to civilian life and important to our men and women in uniform." As the Commission proceeded it was clear that the General was not pleased to have been assigned this particular commission, thinking instead he would have received an appointment to something more prestigious and more worthy of his name. Of note, by his omission it was never called the Herres Commission.

From the beginning of the Commission the General gave me very little direction. So I designed my own course, framing up my staff much similar to what I had done in my navy squadrons. The department heads would become the nucleus of the commission. Concurrently, I surveyed available real estate and leased a spacious suite on the third floor of an older building on Pennsylvania Avenue, several blocks from the Capitol.

I contacted an academically talented lady I had known through the Boeing Company in St. Louis, Missouri. Dr. Kathleen Robertson, PhD, was a lawyer and widow of an Air Force pilot killed during the Vietnam War. She was running a strategy department for the Chief Executive Officer of Boeing and was attracted by my offer to head the Research and Analysis Department for the commission. I arranged with GSA to pay for her move and I had nailed down my first *plank holder*.

Fran and I talked about my new assignment. I was unaware of an important policy when taking the position of Staff Director for the Commission. The policy that I should be using volunteers who supported GOP candidates was made very clear to me in my first few weeks by the Presidential Employment Office. I was told to hire staff from the PEO office in the White House where they had a large pool of young people who volunteered their services to the Republican Presidential campaign. I had begun hiring outside of the Presidential pool and received a call from an official in the PEO office who suggested that I use their pool first. As it turned out, the pool was a wonderful, refreshing and talented reservoir of young people from which to fill out my staff. With the staff complete, the Presidential Commission was off and running.

The other Department Head positions were General Counsel, Communications, Congressional Affairs and Operations and Administration. The total staff complement was comprised of thirty-four full-time staffers and eight part-time interns. In a short time the staff was in place and ready to take directions from Chairman Herres and the presidentially appointed Commissioners.

I was proud to work with this prestigious group. However, the two people with whom I primarily affiliated with were Elaine Donnelly and General Max Thurman. Elaine Donnelly was the most active Commissioner on the Commission and took the tasking on as a full-time job. Most of the Commissioners contributed based upon their backgrounds and exposure to the military and was the primary reason for them to have been appointed by the President.

Elaine Donnelly was clearly on a mission to preclude women from being in combat. She was the head of the Center for Military Readiness, whose goals were to preclude women in combat and gays in the military. One of my most difficult tasks was to ensure that my staff, many of whom had their own views on what results the study should produce, remained completely neutral in the gathering and accumulating of data. Elaine or another Commissioner with a strong penchant for one perspective or the other of a key issue often captured a staffer who was sympathetic to his or her political views and attempted to sway the data. In the end I felt that I was able to deter those types of influences for the most part and the data was as pure as it could be considering the disparate views of the Commissioners.

The Commission report was one hundred and twenty-one pages of issues, discussions and decisions. The *Commission on Alternate Views* were positions by Commissioners that deviated from the majority vote and why. There were over two hundred pages of dissenting views and appendices, including the longest of which was *Physiology*. Next in length was *Surveys and Polls,* then *Fact-finding Trips, Meetings and Witnesses Interviewed, Statements for the Record, Bibliographies* and *Commissioners Biographies.*

The issues that received the most press and public interest were:

- *Women in Ground Combat*: Women should be excluded from direct combat units and positions. Yes: 10; No: 3; Abstention: 2
- *Women in Combat Aircraft*: Prohibiting woman from assignment to duty on aircraft involved in combat missions. Yes: 8; No: 7; Abstention: 0
- *Women in Combatant Vessels*: Repeal existing laws and modify Service policies for servicewomen to serve on combatant vessels except for submarines and amphibious vessels. Yes: 8; No: 6; Abstention: 1

Bud delivered the report to the Old Executive Office Building for the President to review. At the time President George Bush was a lame duck president, and to his knowledge the report was never reviewed by the Clinton Administration.

My role during the time Bud served on the Presidential Commission was enjoyable. We hosted several large dinner parties at our home to encourage discourse. On occasion we met at a restaurant for dinner. Bud was a master at separating conservatives from liberals to ensure everyone had a pleasant evening. I was happy to be included to listen and learn the differing opinions and was careful to stay neutral in my responses.

With the commission behind us I felt comfortable expressing my opinions and clarifying when someone approached me with what they considered to be incorrect recommendations found by the commission. Also, our youngest daughter, Sue, enlisted and served three and one-half years in the Army before returning home to graduate from college with honors. She was smart, athletic and adventuresome and went through boot camp at Fort Jackson, South Carolina, before gender norming was in place. Sue was five foot two and weighed one hundred and five pounds and competed on a level playing field with men, many of whom were over six feet tall and two hundred pounds. As expected, she made it through boot camp and went on to spend three years in Augsburg, Germany, as a radio teletype operator and driver of a big two-and-a-half-ton truck. Her truck pulled a trailer with a generator which was used to provide electricity to command centers in the field. I thought when she was near the French border with her big truck that she was spying on the French. She had six years of French in school, and this was an opportunity for the Army to put her knowledge and language skills to good use. Bud laughed at my thoughts on the subject and said, "The reality was she performed a difficult job in challenging circumstances and did it well. I was happy she had the opportunity of great choices—Army, Navy or Air Force!"

However, as the mother of two daughters I am firm in my position that I do not want my daughters or granddaughters in harm's way. I also wouldn't want our son to be injured or killed attempting to protect a woman who didn't have the physical strength to keep up. The guilt would be unfathomable.

I respect Fran's opinion on this difficult subject. It is not as simple for me. As the Staff Director of the Presidential Commission my charter was to plan and execute hearings for the Commission, and to hire and manage a staff to provide meaningful witnesses from the services to testify before the Commission. In the end my staff would compile a report to the President that reflected the views of the Commissioners who he had appointed for this task.

You will notice that nowhere in my charter did it state what Bud Orr thinks about the subject. To the contrary, one of my most difficult daily responsibilities was to preclude my staff, including myself, from contributing to the decision matrix. This was up to the Commissioners and my staff's role was to record and print it.

Of course I had opinions, particularly regarding women pilots flying in combat. But for the sake of this story I chose to refrain from expressing them. Women in the military now are competing and in many cases winning over their male counterparts. In Naval Aviation women are flying on and off of aircraft carriers day and night, performing all of the warfare specialties and in many cases leading the pack.

There was one issue that, in retrospect, the Commission failed to anticipate. Young women pilots can have high aspirations to compete and win in all aspects of warfare and combat. However, Mother Nature clicks in at a certain point in their lives as was intended, and their desire to procreate takes precedence over career. When mid-career women fighter pilots screen for department head of squadrons and deploy aboard a carrier they often opt for motherhood.

This has caused a significant dip in the population of contenders to move up the line. Although it presents more opportunities for their male counterparts who were once their contenders one could speculate that they might not be the best ones. However, at the very least it causes manual intervention in the assignment process to make up for the vacancies as mid-grade women pilots become moms and drop out of the completion.

As complicated as the process was I was fortunate to be exposed regularly to two-, three- and four-star admirals and generals on the Commission, each of whom were elite leaders and warriors in their services and beyond. One in particular I must single out and give thanks to even though he has passed on is General Maxwell Thurmond. He was a visionary and most remarkable man. General Thurmond led the 1989 invasion of Panama and was the principal architect of the all-volunteer Army. The General would take me aside after a Commissioners hearing and share his views on where we needed to go next. His insights were always instinctively correct, and I will always be grateful to have shared even a moment of his precious time.

Since I am in the thanking mode I'll thank Fran for her remarkable calm and patience during this year-long process. I travelled and was away from home more than I wanted to be. I invited my staff into our home regularly without the first complaint from her. At night after we had gone to bed I would often receive calls from one of the Commissioners. She would often fall asleep and wake up to hear me on the telephone with a different Commissioner who wanted information on one of the issues.

During the process of dismantling the Presidential Commission and the office spaces, I received an intriguing call at home from a three-star Air Force General in the Pentagon. The General was the military assistant to Les Aspin, the powerful former Chairman of the House Armed Services Committee and Secretary of Defense, and he asked me to pay a call on Secretary Aspin the next day. I was flattered and honored to meet personally with the Secretary although I didn't know the reason for the visit.

The following day I arrived for my appointment with the Secretary at his office in the Pentagon. I was escorted in by a General and introduced to Secretary Aspin before being seated. The Secretary said, "Captain Orr, you have done a superb job on the *Presidential Commission on the Assignment of Women in Combat*; however, I'm afraid we are not through with your services. I would like you to run a private study on *Gays in the Military*, reporting directly to my office." Reluctantly, I agreed to take the job because who would ever decline a request from the Secretary of Defense?

Before leaving the Pentagon, the General introduced me to the famous Doc Holiday, who made sure that special people in the Pentagon were properly cared for. He suggested that I have a small cadre of protection during the study time period. Although overwhelmed by the prospect of needing protection, I agreed and headed home to break the news to Fran regarding my new position.

On Sunday we were awakened by an early morning telephone call from the West Coast. "Skipper, this is John Jones. You may not remember me but I served with you in the VA-122 Flying Eagles, when you were the Commanding Officer."

I said, "Of course I remember you, John. You were an excellent officer." John said, "Thank you, sir, but did you ever think I was different?"

I replied, "I seem to recall you always did a good job, were exceptionally fit, well groomed, a bit of a loner and somewhat reclusive."

John replied, "You are correct, sir. I am also gay. The reason for calling is about an article in *USA Today*'s weekend edition. The title of the article is *Former Navy Pilot to Run Secret Gay Study*, and it gave your name. I'm calling you on behalf of my friends. We are concerned that since many of us have retired from the military and have come out that the government may try to take away our benefits."

I was completely taken back by John's news. Before I hung up the phone I let John know I was sympathetic to his concerns and would consider them when I knew more about what the potential study entailed.

I got out of bed, reluctant to leave Fran so early on a Sunday morning. I dressed and left the house to buy a newspaper. Sure enough, when I picked up a copy of *USA Today* I saw the article John had mentioned on the back of page one. The reporter who wrote the article included in the story that I was part of the Tailhook debacle in 1991. That part of the story was totally false because I had been in Hanoi, Vietnam, with Senator McCain during the Tailhook Convention that year.

It was later surmised that Congresswoman Patsy Schroeder, former Congresswoman from Colorado, a known feminist who had been a major thorn in my side during the Presidential Commission, was the source of the article. Furthermore, Congresswoman Schroeder had also sent a Chicago-based newspaper reporter to interview young female staffers whom I had travelled with when I served as the Principle Deputy in the Office of Legislative Affairs. Congresswoman Schroeder attempted to obtain some dirt on me by having the reporter ask the female Senate staffers if I had made sexual advances toward them. Two of the staffers were personal friends of Fran and me. The staffer called me to alert us to the illicit queries. I pulled Fran into my arms and said, "Thank God for the love of *the woman worth pursuing* and leaving my rowdy days behind."

On Monday morning, I received a call from Secretary Aspin's office and was asked if I had seen the article in *USA Today*. I replied, "Yes, sir." The General asked me to come to his office in the Pentagon as soon as possible.

The appointment was just with the General and I didn't see Secretary Aspin again. The General said, "We do not know the source of the leak, but the Secretary no longer will need your services. The Secretary has decided to keep the study within the military, and it will be run by an active-duty Army Colonel in the Pentagon." The General thanked me again for my outstanding service.

I called Fran before leaving the Pentagon. I said, "Franny, I feel an enormous weight has been lifted off my shoulders. I'm on my way home. Are you ready for a new adventure?"

29

Final Flight

A YOUNG FORMER STUDENT OF MINE John (Gucci) Foley contacted me after he was selected to be one of the famous Blue Angels. He asked if I wanted to fly with him during an air show in the two-seat FA-18 Hornet.

When I was the Commanding Officer of VA-122, Flying Eagles, I had flown with Gucci several times and admired his spirit and enthusiasm for Naval Aviation. The Blue Angels were scheduled to perform at Andrews Air Force Base near Washington, D.C., during my term on the Presidential Commission.

Although I had retired from the Navy, I was still on terminal leave and therefore was eligible to fly in a Navy jet. I accepted the invitation and showed up at Andrews in my flight suit, along with the throngs of thousands of air show fans. In the parking lot on the Air Force base I met with the Commanding Officer of the Blue Angels, Commander Greg (Rugdance) Wooldridge. Rugdance was a tall, muscular, suntanned and handsome pilot. He said, "CAG, I know you want to fly with Gucci in his solo position, but I have a suggestion. The solo positions are very aggressive. I flew twice with Gucci in winter training in the desert and was unconscious from the g's most of the flight. Frankly, I was so beaten up and stiff that I couldn't fly for several days both times. Why don't you have a nice comfortable ride in the slot position?" I took another look at Rugdance, rippling with muscles and fifteen years younger and made a good decision. The decision to ride in the slot was an easy one I was happy to have made.

Our take-off was smooth. I was in the back seat of Blue Angel aircraft number four (in the slot) of the diamond flight of four. The two wingmen in the diamond formation flew so close to my aircraft that the wings were inches away from the canopy. Because of my position in the formation of the aircraft I was literally in the shadow of the aircrafts' wings and the tail of Rugdance's lead airplane looked like it was glued to the canopy of my pilot's aircraft.

Each of the formation maneuvers was highly challenging and executed smoothly. However, when the aircrafts broke out of the diamond formation each aircraft separated, going in a different direction as part of the show. My pilot would snap over six g's on the aircraft, causing my head to almost touch my own lap. The Blues flew without the protection of g suits and I was rapidly unconscious for several seconds before the pilot let up on the g's. The aircraft had a video camera mounted over my head that took a video of my face and body during the entire flight. I said, "Anyone who saw the tape knew how embarrassed I was to watch myself bouncing around in the back of the aircraft, in the shadow of the wings and tail of another aircraft, just inches from the cockpit. In the next scene I was flopping around in the cockpit, unconscious with a small drool coming down my lips." Thank God Rugdance made the suggestion for me not to fly with Gucci or I might not have survived.

After an unbelievable ride the Blues landed and taxied into the flight line in typical Blue Angel style, parked side by side and shut down the engines. Much to my surprise when I wobbly climbed down the ladder I saw my staff from the Presidential Commission waiting by the aircraft. They had a very large bucket of ice and water behind them which they later poured over my head. I was honored, and will never forget the memorable flight or the wonderful group of patriots on my staff who served in a political dimension.

It has been nearly two decades since my *Final Flight* and I look back fondly on all those years of flying and the wonderful friends we had made. Since leaving the Navy we have remained in our wonderful nation's capital and I have worked for companies closely associated with aerospace and Naval Aviation as a government relations specialist. Fran continues her steadfast support of all of my adventures, and all my travels, while offering invaluable support, stability and counsel to our family.

Although the business world has brought new expanded opportunities, risks and rewards there has been a distinct lack of the reciprocal camaraderie and allegiance that we experienced while serving in the Navy. There is no more anticipation of flight, no more night catapult shots, no more close calls with death but also none of the unparalleled unity and sense of trust.

The Navy family bonds us together unequivocally. Many factors determine how long we can serve, and we usually know when the time comes to move on. But while moving on we welcome a new set of opportunities with their own challenges, risks and rewards and will let the hardships of the past stay tucked away. Our marriage has never been Pollyannaish but in the aggregate we have been blessed by experiences that few people in the world ever encounter. Fran acknowledges and encourages my whims, but more than ever takes the lead. We have replaced an aircraft carrier and associated thrills with a boat of our own and found a whole new culture of people who love boating and the water. We have found an oasis of people who share a unique fraternity of seeking adventure on the water. Most weekends will find us cruising up the Potomac River to Georgetown or down the river to Old Town Alexandria. Life doesn't get better than a spending a Fourth of July watching glorious fireworks over the Washington Monument while sitting on our boat. There are times we cruise down the river past Mount Vernon, the home of George Washington. In the summer we continue our travels into the Chesapeake Bay and also into the Atlantic Ocean and on to Virginia Beach. Fran and I look at each other in wonder at all the mystery and magic we have discovered together. "For now we wish you fair winds and following seas."

Epilogue
Charlie on Arrival

I don't know the genesis of the term *Charlie on Arrival*. I do know the term *Charlie on Arrival* is used on an aircraft carrier to let incoming aircraft know the flight deck is prepared and aircraft are cleared into the landing pattern. Now! Right now! In the broadest sense *Charlie on Arrival* means "We are ready for you. Welcome home."

In the context of this book, I ask that you picture yourself all alone in a jet fighter. You are flying on a crystal clear sky-blue day, streaking across the ocean. As you look out of your cockpit you see one of our country's most treasured possessions cruising quietly at nearly thirty miles per hour. The aircraft carrier is pushing ninety thousand tons of steel, nearly a hundred aircraft with five thousand men onboard through bright emerald-green water. The carrier leaves behind a tidal wave–sized wake with no shore to wash upon.

Within the silence of your jet you key the mike and say, "Climax, Battlecry three zero one is forty-five miles from mother with a flight of four."

The response comes back, in a voice as clear as God himself, "Roger three zero one you are *Charlie on Arrival*."

You gently lower the pointed nose of your jet and direct it toward the stern of the carrier as your three wingmen close in so tight you feel like one aircraft, one body. You level off at six hundred feet above the water, travelling at four hundred miles per hour, and feel the exhilaration only few experience in a lifetime. You cross the stern and roll quickly into a ninety-degree bank easing on four g's. Next, you pull back the power with the nose of the aircraft on the horizon and decelerate to drop the landing gear and flaps. The tailhook is already down. Silently, you carve into the groove, the glide path on centerline, and see the ever-welcome yellow *meatball* flanked by rows of green lights telling you, "You are right on glide path."

Now you see the brief flash of the green power lights on the top of the lens activated by the landing signal officer, a signal that you are cleared to land. Every muscle and brain cell in your body smoothly coordinates with the throttles, the engines and the flight controls to bring your single-seat jet across the fantail to a perfect number three wire landing. Immediately, you slam the throttles to full power as the arrestment throws you forward, with your torso harness holding you tight into your ejection seat. The aircraft comes to a violent stop with the engines at full power. Immediately you go to idle. What an incredible rush!

Fran and I wish to dedicate this book to all who have heard *Charlie on Arrival* early in life like some of our friends in this book: Whiskey-Man, Jessie, Admiral Smith, the young yellow-shirt petty officer who got the call in stormy seas as he was thrown against the nose wheel of my Harrier on the flight deck and, most recently, our beloved friend, former Top Gun Commanding Officer Chris (Boomer) Wilson.

We will all get *the call* sooner or later. But those who wear the Navy Wings of Gold know the glory of *Charlie on Arrival.* For it is by catapulting off of and landing aboard an aircraft carrier that this unique band of brothers carry within them a picture perfect vision of reaching out to touch the hand of God.

Glossary

A-4 Skyhawk—a single-seat light-attack jet designed by McDonnell Douglas that was the workhorse of the Navy during the Vietnam War

Air Boss—head Air Department officer on aircraft carrier

Air taxi—to hover fore and aft

Alpha strike—multiple aircraft strike on a target

AV-8A Harrier—a single-seat, short take-off vertical landing aircraft with a Rolls-Royce Pegasus engine, designed by Hawker Sidley

Big E—*USS Enterprise*, the first nuclear-powered aircraft carrier

Blue Angels—Navy flight demonstration team

Blue shirt—chocks and ties down aircraft and removes the chains from aircraft on the flight deck

Bolter—failing to engage any of the four arresting wires on aircraft carrier during an attempted carrier landing.

Boom—Type of in-flight refueling done by the USAF

BOQ—Bachelor Officer Quarters

CAG—Carrier Airwing Group Commander

Call sign—nickname of an aviator, chosen by his squadron mates

Carqual—carrier qualifications (CQ)

Catapult grip—the T handle stored in front of the throttles; when lifted up the pilot holds throttles forward during a catapult shot

CATTC—Carrier Air Traffic Control Center

CNO—Chief of Naval Operations

CO—Commanding Officer of a squadron or ship

Collective—helicopter pilot uses this long handle with his left hand to do demand lift from the rotors

Death Machine—AV-8A Harrier

F-8 Crusader—single-seat fighter aircraft

F-14—Grumman Tomcat, two-seat fighter jet, made famous by the movie *Top Gun*

Feet wet—when aircraft cross the beach from the land to the ocean

Fly aboard pilot—pilot who flies aircraft from an air station and land aboard an aircraft carrier during carrier qualifications

Fo'c'sle—anchor chain storage on 0-3 level, in the bow of the aircraft carrier; also used for religious services

FOD—Foreign Object Damage

Fresnel lens—optical landing system on port side of flight deck

Green shirt—catapult and arresting gear crew

Hot switch—pilot who will fly aircraft flown by another pilot who will switch places with him with engines turning

HUD—Heads-up display

JAG—Judge Advocate General

Jarheads—slang name for Marines

JBD—Jet Blast Deflector

LCDR—Navy Lieutenant Commander

LPH—Landing Platform Helicopter

LSO—Landing Signal Officer

Meatball—yellow center ball landing aid

Glossary

Must pump—pilot sent directly from flight training to combat operations

Pitch-Roll-Yaw—aerodynamic parameters of all aircraft

Plane captain—brown shirts that are junior enlisted men responsible for pre- and post-flight of aircraft as well as strapping pilots in the cockpit

Plat—Pilot Landing Aid Television

Poopy suit—cold weather rubber suit

Pri-Fly—Primary flight control tower on an aircraft carrier

Probe and drogue—in-flight refueling done by Navy aircraft

RAG—Replacement Air Group, which trains aviators in fleet aircraft

Ready room—briefing room for squadron pilots and gathering spot during off-duty hours

Red shirt—Ordinance man

RESCAP—Rescue combat control air patrol

Reverse thrust—used in Harrier to vector thrust forward to slow down during or after landing

RIO—Radar Intercept Officer, located in back seat of F-14

Skipper—name for the Commanding Officer of a Navy or Marine squadron, also called CO

Snubber pressure—pneumatic pressure which holds the hook down while landing

Soft hook—tailhook that has lost snubber pressure to hold it down during an arrested landing

Stateroom—officer berthing cabin

STOVL—Short take-off/vertical landing

Transverse g's—gravitational forces applied to the front of the body

Traps—carrier arrested landing on an aircraft carrier

Wardroom—officer dining room on an aircraft carrier

Westpac—Western Pacific ocean

Wing-wash—meant Harrier was depleting wing-lift

XO—Executive Officer or number two in a squadron or ship

Yankee Station—Designated station in the Tonkin Gulf where carriers were located during the Vietnam War

Yellow shirt—airman who directs aircraft on flight deck

Acknowledgments

We wish to thank each of you for taking the time to read *Love at First Flight* and sharing it with family and friends. We are grateful for the many kind endorsements including Senator John McCain, Bud's former flight instructor and author of several best sellers; Captain Gene Cernan, Naval aviator and author of *The Last Man on the Moon*; H. Lawrence Garrett III, the 68th Secretary of the Navy and former corporate executive; Dave (Bio) Baranek, retired Naval Aviator and author of *Top Gun Days*; and Barry Zlatoper, wife of Admiral (Zap) Zlatoper and author of *29 Kitchens*.

We owe a special thanks to our family for their continued support and, after reading our first draft, encouraged us to press on. Our granddaughter, Emily chose the title, and our Editor endorsed it. Our good friend Donna Turner spent countless hours working her "grammatical wizardry" and counseling us on sensitive issues.

A personal thanks is extended to the American people whose tax dollars provide funding for our magnificent aircraft carriers and their accompanied aircraft. Our military system is ready 24-7 to project power around the world in defense of our country and allies. Thank you for entrusting Bud to fly all of the incredible jets you read about in *Love at First Flight*.

We are grateful for the stewardship and guidance from our highly experienced editor, Hillel Black and the publishing team of Robert Astle and Tony Viardo at Astor + Blue Editions. We have been fortunate to have the first team on our side.

We took the liberty of changing a few names for personal reasons. Any errors, omissions, or embellishments can be blamed on an old carrier pilot and his wife's recollection of an awesome journey.

We are one military family among many who have been honored to serve our country in war and peacetime. We will be forever grateful for all of the men and women who have taken up the gauntlet and continue to serve and protect our country from this new emerging threat to our society and life as we have know it. God bless them and God bless America.

Praise for *Love at First Flight*

"Without a doubt—including landing on the moon—a night carrier landing—when it's only you and your maker—when good is not good enough—when a little arrogance helps—when you know you can do it better than it's ever been done before—yet tempered by knowledge that in fact you are not infallible. Being a Naval Aviator means you had better plan on being the best or find something else to do! That's the meaning behind those 'Wings of Gold'—The life of a Naval Aviator by Bud and Fran Orr is vividly depicted in *Love at First Flight*."

—Captain Gene Cernan, author of *The Last Man on the Moon*

"Bud and Fran, by sharing both sides of 'their story,' capture the heart and soul of a fascinating and shared military career. They humorously demonstrate the need for camaraderie, courage, ingenuity, and discipline, along with pure love for the people surrounding them and these gripping stories are honest to God, true. You can't make this stuff up."

—Barry O. Zlatoper, author and photographer of *29 Kitchens, One Cook*, and a Naval aviator's wife

"*Love at First Flight* will grab hold of you and not let you go. Naval Aviation is the exciting backdrop for this intoxicating love story. I witnessed this compelling true tale firsthand when Bud was the commanding officer of my husband's squadron. This amazing story needs to be told and is a great read. You won't be able to put it down."

—Marcia Hinds, author of *I Know You're in There: Our War with Autism* and a Navy wife

"*Love at First Flight—Adventures, Exploits, Sacrifices, Risks and Rewards* is a fascinating look at one of the most interesting characters in naval aviation history. And as we all know, behind every great man and his career, is an equally great and talented woman. Fran has been the glue that has held it all together. This is the story that will define the naval aviation experience. A must read!"

—Ed Bouillianne, author of *You Can't Out Source Weight Loss*